ADULT READING SERIES

Challenger

Teacher's Manual

FOR BOOK 6

COREA MURPHY

ISBN 0-88336-793-9

EACH ONE TEACH ONE

© 1988
New Readers Press
Publishing Division of Laubach Literacy International
Box 131, Syracuse, New York 13210

Printed in the United States of America

Cover design by Chris Steenwerth

9 8 7 6

About the Author

Corea Murphy has worked in the field of education since the early 1960s. In addition to classroom and tutorial teaching, Ms. Murphy has developed language arts curriculum guides for public high schools, conducted curriculum and effectiveness workshops, and established an educational program for residents in a drug rehabilitation facility.

Ms. Murphy became interested in creating a reading series for older students when she began working with adults and adolescents in the early 1970s. The **Challenger Adult Reading Series** is the result of her work with these students.

In a very real sense, the students contributed greatly to the development of this reading series. Their enthusiasm for learning to read and their willingness to work hard provided inspiration, and their many helpful suggestions influenced the content of both the student books and the teacher's manuals.

It is to these students that the **Challenger Adult Reading Series** is dedicated with the hope that others who wish to become good readers will find this reading program both helpful and stimulating.

A special note of gratitude is also extended to Kay Koschnick, Christina Jagger, and Mary Hutchison of New Readers Press for their work and support in guiding this series to completion.

Table of Contents

Introduction to the *Challenger* Series

The *Challenger Adult Reading Series* is a program designed to develop reading, writing, and reasoning skills in adult and adolescent students. The first four books in the *Challenger* series emphasize *learning to read,* developing basic decoding, vocabulary, comprehension, and writing skills. Beginning with Book 5, the emphasis shifts to *reading to learn,* developing higher-level comprehension and reasoning skills while expanding the student's knowledge base.

Components of the Series

The *Challenger* series contains:
- 8 student books
- 5 teacher's manuals
- answer keys for Books 1–4 and 5–8
- the *Challenger Placement Tool*
- 8 puzzle books correlated to the student books
- 4 books of writing activities correlated to Books 1–4

The Student Books

Each book in this controlled vocabulary series contains 20 lessons, plus reviews. Each lesson includes:
- word study
- a reading selection
- a wide variety of exercises and activities

In Books 1, 3, 5, and 7, each lesson begins with a word chart that introduces new words according to specific phonics principles. In all books, new words that appear in the lesson are listed before each reading selection.

The reading selections in the odd-numbered books are mostly fiction. Books 1 and 3 contain original stories about a group of adults in a variety of situations. Most reading selections in Books 5 and 7 are minimally adapted well-known works of fiction. The even-numbered books contain engaging informational readings. The selections in Books 2 and 4 are on topics similar to those in magazines and encyclopedias. Most selections in Books 6 and 8 are adapted from highly respected works of nonfiction that enable students to broaden the scope of their knowledge.

The varied exercises and activities help students to develop their reading, writing, speaking, and listening skills and to increase their basic knowledge. Comprehension exercises based on the reading selections focus on the development of literal, inferential, and applied comprehension skills. In addition, comprehension exercises in Books 5 through 8 develop lit-erary understanding, interpretation, and critical reading skills.

Other exercises are designed to increase vocabulary and develop reading and reasoning skills. They include vocabulary reviews; word associations; classifying, sequencing, and categorizing exercises; using context clues; forming analogies; using dictionaries and reference materials; and several types of puzzles.

There are reviews after every four or five lessons, except in Books 1 and 3. Each book has a final review. Also included in Books 1 through 5 are indexes of the words introduced so far in that book. The word indexes for Books 6 through 8 are included in the teacher's manuals. These word indexes can be used in developing reinforcement activities and vocabulary reviews.

The Teacher's Manuals

There is a single *Teacher's Manual for Books 1–4* and individual teacher's manuals for Books 5, 6, 7, and 8. These comprehensive manuals explain the concepts underlying the *Challenger* series and offer practical suggestions about procedures and techniques for working with students. Separate chapters deal with preparing to teach, teaching the lessons, writing, reinforcement activities, and using the lesson notes. These chapters should be read before you begin to use this program. Individual lesson notes containing suggestions for pre-reading, post-reading, and writing activities, and comments on specific exercises should be read before teaching the lessons. In the teacher's manuals, there are also introductions to each book, scope and sequence charts, and answer keys for each book. Finally, the *Teacher's Manual for Books 1–4* contains a chart of the common phonics principles and elements in English words.

Student Writing

Students are encouraged to write from the very first lesson. Early in the series, exercises focus on writing at the sentence level and are designed to simultaneously improve spelling, sentence structure, and students' skill in expressing themselves clearly. Most lessons in Books 5 through 8 have exercises that require students to write brief paragraphs. Suggestions for providing additional writing activities are given in the individual lesson notes.

Significant Educational Features

Flexibility and Adaptability

The *Challenger* series has been used successfully with students in many different types of instructional settings:
- adult volunteer literacy programs
- ABE, pre-GED, and GED programs
- secondary remedial reading programs
- secondary special education programs
- community college reading programs
- educational programs in correctional institutions
- workforce tutorial programs for employees

Challenger can be used in one-to-one tutoring situations, as well as in a variety of group settings. The lessons can be adapted to fit a variety of formats, allowing you to introduce additional activities and topics related to individual student interests and needs.

An Integrated Approach

Challenger integrates reading, writing, speaking, and listening skills. Reading comprehension is developed through oral discussion of inferential- and applied-level questions. These discussions help students to develop speaking and listening skills. Students build writing skills through follow-up writing activities. Critical thinking and reasoning skills are developed as students discuss the readings, the exercises, and their writing activities.

Sequenced Skill Building

Each lesson builds upon the skills developed and the content introduced in previous lessons. Students are continually challenged as the lessons increase in length and difficulty. As reading selections become longer, the content, vocabulary, and sentence structure become more sophisticated and demanding. The exercises and writing activities build on and expand students' knowledge and abilities. Students experience a sense of progress as they learn to apply their skills to new situations.

Highly Motivating Material

Students who have used the *Challenger* series have commented that this reading program has many characteristics that help to hold their interest and maintain their motivation. The characteristics they most frequently cite include:
- exceptionally motivating reading selections
- mature and diverse material
- information that increases background knowledge
- emphasis on using reasoning powers
- challenge of increasingly difficult materials
- feelings of success and confidence generated by the program

Placement

The *Challenger Placement Tool,* used in conjunction with information you have about a student's background knowledge, speaking and writing abilities, and motivation, can help you to decide where to place the student in the *Challenger* series. Scores on standardized reading inventories can also be used. For the first four books, scores in the following reading level ranges are appropriate:

Book 1: 2.0	**Book 3:** 3.0–4.5
Book 2: 2.0–3.0	**Book 4:** 4.0–5.0

Keep in mind that numerical reading levels by themselves are not adequate descriptors of adult reading abilities. For students already using the series, scoring 85 per cent or better on the final review in each book indicates that the student is ready to go on to the next book.

Although it is recognized that there are students of both sexes, for the sake of clarity and simplicity, we chose to use the pronouns *he, him,* and *his* throughout this book.

SCOPE AND SEQUENCE: BOOK 6

Word Analysis — Lesson	1	2	3	4	5	R	6	7	8	9	10	R	11	12	13	14	15	R	16	17	18	19	20	R
1. Use syllabication to decode words	☆	☆	☆	☆	☆	☆	☆	☆	☆	☆	☆	☆	☆	☆	☆	☆	☆	☆	☆	☆	☆	☆	☆	☆
2. Recognize word families					☆			☆														☆		
3. Form compound words									☆			☆				☆								
4. Recognize/form abbreviations										☆		☆									☆			☆
5. Recognize/form contractions	☆							☆	☆				☆	☆				☆						
6. Form/use words with common suffixes:																								
-ment	☆										☆													
-ness		☆	☆	☆		☆					☆													
-or			☆																					
-ly						☆			☆	☆	☆													
-ence/-ance						☆															☆			
-tion						☆													☆					
-ful							☆		☆		☆													
-less						☆	☆																	
-sion											☆													
-ize																				☆			☆	
7. Recognize/use common prefixes:																								
un-													☆											
il-														☆	☆									
im-															☆									
in-															☆									
ir-															☆									
non-															☆	☆								
re-																	☆							
pre-																								

Vocabulary — Lesson	1	2	3	4	5	R	6	7	8	9	10	R	11	12	13	14	15	R	16	17	18	19	20	R
1. Learn unfamiliar vocabulary	★	★	★	★	★	★	★	★	★	★	★	★	★	★	★	★	★	★	★	★	★	★	★	★
2. Infer word meanings from context clues	★	☆	★	★	★	☆	☆	☆	☆	☆	★	☆	☆	★	★	★	☆	☆	★	☆	☆	☆	★	☆
3. Identify definitions/descriptions of terms					☆	★	★	☆	☆	☆	☆	★	☆	★	★	★	★	★	★		★	☆	☆	★
4. Identify synonyms			★	★		★	★					★	★				★				★			
5. Identify antonyms			★	★		★			☆			★	★			★	★				★			
6. Form/use compound words					☆			★	☆			★								☆				
7. Identify symbols											★			☆						☆		☆		★
8. Complete analogies												☆						☆						
9. Complete word associations	☆	☆						☆		☆		☆						☆				☆	☆	
10. Complete word puzzles																							☆	
11. Learn/review sayings and idiomatic expressions								☆		☆		☆			☆						★		☆	

Key: ★ = Primary emphasis   ☆ = Secondary emphasis   ☆ = Integrated with other skills

Comprehension

Lesson	1	2	3	4	5	R	6	7	8	9	10	R	11	12	13	14	15	R	16	17	18	19	20	R
1. Read selections independently	★	★	★	★	★		★	★	★	★	★	★	★	★	★	★	★		★	★	★	★	★	★
2. Complete exercises independently	★	★	★	★	★	★	★	★	★	★	★	★	★	★	★	★	★	★	★	★	★	★	★	★
3. Identify words using context clues	★	★	★	★	★	★	★	★	★	★	★	★	★	★	★	★	★	★	★	★	★	★	★	★
4. Improve listening comprehension	☆	☆	☆	☆	☆	☆	☆	☆	☆	☆	☆	☆	☆	☆	☆	☆	☆	☆	☆	☆	☆	☆	☆	☆
5. Improve oral reading	☆	☆	☆	☆	☆	☆	☆	☆	☆	☆	☆	☆	☆	☆	☆	☆	☆	☆	☆	☆	☆	☆	☆	☆
6. Develop literal comprehension skills:																								
- Recall details	★	★	★	★	★	★	★	★	★	★	★	★	★	★	★	★	★	★	★	★	★	★	★	★
- Locate specific information	★	★	★	★	★	★	★	★	★	★	★	★	★	★	★	★	★	★	★	★	★	★	★	★
7. Develop inferential comprehension skills:																								
- Support statements with appropriate details	★	★		★	★		★	★	★	★	★	★	★	★	★		★		★	★	★	★	★	
- Infer word meanings from context clues	★	☆	★	★	★	☆	☆	☆	☆	☆	★	☆	★	★	★	★	☆	☆	★	☆	☆	☆	★	☆
- Use context clues to fill in missing words	★	☆	☆	★	★	☆	☆	☆	☆	☆	☆	☆	★	☆	☆	★	☆	★	☆	☆	☆	★	★	★
- Infer information from reading	☆	☆	☆	★	★		☆	☆	☆	☆	☆	☆	☆	☆	☆	☆	☆		☆	☆	☆	☆	☆	
- Draw conclusions based on reading				☆						★	☆	☆	☆		☆						☆	☆		
- Identify/infer cause & effect relationships				☆	★		☆	☆					★									★		
- Distinguish between positive & negative statements										★														
- Classify words under topic headings										★							☆	★				★		
- Distinguish between fact & opinion							★									★	★	★						★
- Translate Middle English						☆													☆					
8. Develop applied comprehension skills:																								
- Draw conclusions based on personal experience	★	★							★		★	★	☆	★	★	★	★	★	★	★		☆	☆	
- Relate reading to personal experience							★	★	★	☆	★	☆	★	★	★	★	★	★		★	★	★		
9. Locate/review basic factual information	☆	☆				☆	☆	☆	☆	★	☆	☆	☆	☆	☆	☆	★	☆		★	☆	☆	☆	☆
10. Locate/infer information from:																								
- classified ads						★		★																
- diagram									☆															
- travel brochure												☆	☆											
- driver's test													☆											
- editorial cartoon															★									
- calorie chart																			★					

Key: ★ = Primary emphasis   ☆ = Secondary emphasis   ☆ = Integrated with other skills

10

Literary Understanding

Lesson	1	2	3	4	5	R	6	7	8	9	10	R	11	12	13	14	15	R	16	17	18	19	20	R
1. Distinguish between fiction and nonfiction	☆	☆	☆	☆	☆	☆	☆	☆	☆	☆	☆	☆	☆	☆	☆	☆	☆	☆	☆	☆	☆	☆	☆	☆
2. Identify/interpret characters' actions, motivations, feelings, and qualities			★	★	★		☆	☆			★				★	☆					★		★	
3. Identify/interpret plot/setting				★	★					★	★													
4. Predict outcome					★																★		★	
5. Interpret poetry															★						★			
6. Interpret drama																								
7. Recognize autobiography		☆			☆								☆			☆								
8. Recognize biography		☆						☆							☆	☆							☆	
9. Relate to characters' motivations & feelings				☆	☆		☆				☆		☆		☆	☆					★		☆	
10. Infer author's attitude toward material						★		☆		☆	☆		★		☆	☆					☆		☆	☆

Writing

Lesson	1	2	3	4	5	R	6	7	8	9	10	R	11	12	13	14	15	R	16	17	18	19	20	R
1. Write sentence or paragraph answers to questions	★	★	☆	★	★	☆	★	★	★	★	★	★	★	★	★	★	★	★	★	★	★	★	★	★
2. Form a reasoned opinion	★	★	☆	★	★	☆	★	★	★	★	★	★	★	★	★	★	★	★	★	☆	★	★	★	★
3. Copy words accurately	☆	☆	☆	☆	☆	☆	☆	☆	☆	☆	☆	☆	☆	☆	☆	☆	☆	☆	☆	☆	☆	☆	☆	☆
4. Fill out a job application										★														
5. Spelling:																								
- Form the plural of words ending in *f* or *fe*	☆																							
- Change *y* to *i* before adding suffix			☆	☆					☆		☆													
- Use an apostrophe to show ownership															☆	☆		☆	☆	☆	☆		☆	
- Spell words with greater accuracy	☆	☆	☆	☆	☆	☆	☆	☆	☆	☆	☆	☆	☆	☆	☆	☆	☆	☆	☆	☆	☆	☆	☆	☆
- Learn capitalization rules			☆	☆					☆															
- Capitalize words appropriately	☆	☆	☆	☆	☆	★	☆	☆	☆	☆	☆	★	☆	☆	☆	☆	☆	☆	☆	☆	☆	☆	☆	☆

Note: Specific suggestions for additional writing assignments appear in the individual lesson notes and in Chapter 5 of this manual.

Study Skills

Lesson	1	2	3	4	5	R	6	7	8	9	10	R	11	12	13	14	15	R	16	17	18	19	20	R
1. Increase concentration	☆	☆	☆	☆	☆	☆	☆	☆	☆	☆	☆	☆	☆	☆	☆	☆	☆	☆	☆	☆	☆	☆	☆	☆
2. Skim selection to locate information	☆	☆	☆	☆	☆	☆	☆	☆	☆	☆	☆	☆	☆	☆	☆	☆	☆	☆	☆	☆	☆	☆	☆	☆
3. Apply reasoning skills to exercises:																								
- context clues	★	☆	★	★	★	☆	☆	☆	☆	★	☆	☆	☆	★	★	★	☆	☆	★	☆	★	☆	★	☆
- process of elimination	☆	☆	☆	☆	☆	☆	☆	☆	☆	☆	☆	☆	☆	☆	☆	☆	☆	☆	☆	☆	☆	☆	☆	☆
- "intelligent guessing"	☆	☆	☆	☆	☆	☆	☆	☆	☆	☆	☆	☆	☆	☆	☆	☆	☆	☆	☆	☆	☆	☆	☆	☆
4. Use a dictionary:																								
- to look up word meanings	☆	☆				☆			☆		☆	☆	☆	☆	☆	☆	☆	☆	☆	☆	☆	☆	☆	☆
- to form compound words																☆								
5. Use reference materials:																								
- to identify bodies of water																	★							
- to identify state capitals		☆																						

Key: ★ = Primary emphasis   ☆ = Secondary emphasis   ☆ = Integrated with other skills

11

1. Introduction to Book 6

The format of Book 6 corresponds to the one used in Books 2 and 4. Book 6 introduces relatively few new words and concepts in order to give students the opportunity to thoroughly review and reinforce vocabulary and reasoning skills and further develop their reading comprehension. Capitalization rules and the proper use of the apostrophe represent the major new skills emphasized in this book.

The readings for Book 6 are, for the most part, nonfiction selections which have been minimally adapted from works of widely-acclaimed writers. Experience indicates that motivation and self-esteem are bolstered when students are made aware of this fact. Adult students should also be made aware that the GED Test includes brief, nonfiction passages with accompanying questions. In working with the readings in Book 6, adults often become increasingly confident of their ability to achieve this long-range educational goal.

A review appears after every five lessons. These reviews provide students with additional opportunities to review words and concepts. They also help students develop the habit of referring to previous lessons for the correct answers to some of the questions.

Book 6 is generally used by students who have completed Book 5 in this series. Book 6 is also an appropriate starting place for students who score in the 6.5-7.5 range on standardized reading achievement tests. The final review in Book 5 can also be used as a diagnostic tool. An accuracy rate of 85% or better for this review indicates that students are ready for Book 6.

Students who start this series in Book 6 may need oral reading practice. This is because many students who begin their work at this level either lack confidence or are simply careless readers. Often their homework reflects carelessness, also. By gently calling students' attention to oral reading errors and conducting homework critiques, you can help students correct this pattern.

Book 6 builds upon procedures and practices emphasized in the earlier books in this series. Thus, you may find it worthwhile to look through the manual notes for the previous books.

Scheduling Considerations

Book 6 works well in a classroom setting. The most progress is achieved when students work with *Challenger* a minimum of 45 minutes two or three times a week. Students can work independently, in a group, or with a partner. When working with other students, they receive the support and stimulation from one another that makes learning more enjoyable. Also, the more advanced students can assume much of the responsibility for giving explanations and leading reinforcement activities, which

in turn reinforces their own reading skills. Experience indicates that less advanced students usually benefit from peer instruction provided that you are available to supply any necessary clarifications.

The Lesson Components

Later chapters of this manual outline the principles and procedures that form the foundation of this reading series. The major components of the lessons in Book 6 are briefly described below.

Words for Study

This section, which precedes the reading selection in each lesson, lists words in the lesson that appear for the first time in this series. As was the case in the earlier books, these words appear in the same order and form in which they initially appear in the lesson. This gives students additional practice in pronouncing word endings accurately.

The Reading Selection

The readings for Book 6 have been organized into four units: The Movies, Work, Going Places, and Food. Although a work of fiction has been included in each of these units, the emphasis is on nonfiction. Because some students still have difficulty distinguishing fiction from nonfiction, these terms should be mentioned when appropriate. You will also have the occasion to review the terms *biography* and *autobiography*. Keep these reviews short and simple. Terminology is best understood when it is presented in small, repeated doses.

All initial readings, with the possible exception of the first lesson, are to be done as homework activities.

About the Reading

The comprehension questions call for a variety of different responses: multiple choice, fill-in-the-blank, and complete sentence responses. This variety gives students practice with formats that appear on both job-placement tests and the GED Test—two exams that many students using this book may well encounter.

Other Exercises

A wide variety of exercises has been included to help students improve their recall, increase their vocabulary, and develop their reasoning abilities. As often as seems appropriate, draw the students' attention to the fact that reasoning is an essential part of reading. Help them develop such patterns as using the process of elimination, making intelligent guesses, using the dictionary, and referring to previous lessons when completing these exercises.

A score of 80% or higher should be considered satisfactory on these exercises. If students consistently score below this figure, take some time to help them pinpoint the problem. Generally, they are trying to complete the exercises too rapidly.

Because students are encouraged to learn from their mistakes, they should not be penalized for making them. If you work in a school which gives report cards, it is strongly recommended that evaluations be based on corrected work and overall progress rather than on students' initial efforts. In no way does this practice encourage typical reading students to be careless in completing their homework. Rather they usually become more interested in reading than in report cards, they are more relaxed and patient with themselves in completing assignments, and they develop a more realistic definition of academic progress.

Reinforcement Activities

Suggestions and procedures for reinforcement activities for those words and concepts that give students difficulty are discussed in Chapter 4.

Writing Assignments

Student writing is discussed in Chapter 5. It is recommended that students working in Book 6 complete weekly writing assignments in addition to the writing that is required to complete the exercises in the individual lessons. Suggestions for writing assignments are given in the individual lesson notes.

Paragraphs or brief essays about discussion topics that interest students and personal and/or business letters are appropriate writing assignments. The recommended length for writing assignments is 150-300 words. If students are capable of writing longer compositions and are eager to do so, by all means let them.

The Lesson Format

The procedure for each lesson should be as consistent as possible.

1. Students go over the writing assignment if one was given and review the work in the previous lesson first. This includes discussing the reading selection and correcting the exercises.
2. If time permits, students complete relevant reinforcement activities. The nature and scope of these activities are determined by the needs of your students and how often you meet with them.
3. Students preview the next lesson, which is usually assigned for homework.

Individual Lesson Notes

Lesson notes for each individual lesson appear in Chapter 7 of this manual. These notes contain suggestions and procedures for specific items in each lesson.

Answer Key

An answer key for all the exercises in each lesson of Book 6 follows the lesson notes.

Word Indexes

The word indexes at the back of this manual contain lists of words that are introduced to this series in each unit of Book 6. There is also a master list of all the words introduced in this book. These lists are helpful when developing reinforcement activities. Students may also want to consult these lists periodically.

The next three chapters give suggestions for preparing and teaching the lessons and selecting reinforcement activities.

2. Preparing to Teach

The following suggestions are based on the author's experiences and those of other teachers who have used these books. You may find that your own situation renders some of these suggestions either impractical or impossible to implement in your classroom. It is hoped, however, that most of these suggestions can be modified to meet your particular needs.

How Often to Use *Challenger*

In general, it is recommended that teachers use *Challenger* with students two or three times a week for at least 45 minutes per session. If you meet five times a week with pre-GED students who are eager to pass the tests and have time outside the classroom to complete homework assignments, you may want to use *Challenger* every day.

If you meet five times a week with an adult or adolescent reading class that does not have a specific task such as GED preparation to motivate them, the recommended schedule is to focus on the lessons three times a week and devote the other two class sessions to activities which reinforce or enrich material presented in the lessons. Suggestions about these reinforcement activities appear in Chapter 4.

It is important that students recognize the need to work with *Challenger* regularly. This is often an issue for students in volunteer programs or institutions in which class attendance is not mandatory. Whatever the situation, if a student chooses to attend class on a highly infrequent basis, tell him politely but frankly that there is little point in his attending at all because he's not giving himself a chance to make any significant progress.

If only one class meeting a week is possible, try to schedule this class for 90 minutes to two hours. Also, have the students complete two lessons and, if appropriate, a writing activity for homework. When the students look at you as if you were crazy, show them that by completing a few components of the lessons each day, they will not only be able to do the work, but also reinforce what they are learning. Sports and music are helpful analogies because most students know that both require daily practice.

The Lesson Format

After the first class, which of course involves no homework review, the procedure for each lesson is basically the same. The overview below gives you an idea of what happens during each class. More detailed procedures for this work appear in later chapters of this manual.

1. **Writing assignment.** If students have been given a writing assignment, begin the class by letting them share their work in pairs or small groups. Chapter 5 gives details on writing assignments.

2. **Homework review.** Discuss the reading selection to make sure students have understood it and to give them a chance to react to the reading. Then go over the comprehension questions and the other exercises and have students make any necessary corrections.

3. **Reinforcement activity.** If no writing assignment was given and if time permits, have the students do one or more reinforcement activities. See Chapter 4 for suggestions about reinforcement activities.

4. **Homework preview.** Go over the Words for Study listed at the beginning of the lesson. Introduce the reading selection and call attention to any special features that may be new or confusing. Have students quickly preview the individual exercises for anything they don't understand.

Following this general procedure on a fairly consistent basis helps students because they tend to feel more relaxed and work better when they have a sense of routine. Modifications in the procedure should be made only when they will enhance students' reading development.

Just as you encourage students to see homework assignments as daily workouts, encourage them to see class time as a daily workout, also. These lessons should not be seen as achievement tests but rather as opportunities to move students smoothly toward their reading goals. Students do not have to demonstrate mastery of the material in one lesson in order to go on to the next lesson. Mastery will come with consistent practice.

It is crucial for teachers to think in terms of improvement rather than mastery because students using these books often want to add a fourth component to the lesson format—rationalizing and/or lamenting their mistakes. This uses up valuable classroom time and, if allowed a foothold, will result in students' giving up and dropping out. Students must learn to perceive their mistakes as a natural and helpful part of the learning process. They can learn this only by your gentle but firm reminder that consistent practice is the key to mastery.

Remember that both adult and adolescent reading students tend to be overly sensitive to mistakes in their work. In most cases, they firmly believe that if they hadn't made so many mistakes in the first place, they wouldn't have to be working in these books. For example, a woman in her mid-twenties who decided to quit class explained her reason this way: "My teacher told me that it was all right to make mistakes, but every time I had one in my work she would kind of close her eyes and shake her head like I should have learned all this in the fourth grade." Teachers must think and act in terms of improvement rather than mastery and regard mistakes as natural and helpful.

Do not expect to know at the outset how much time to allot to each segment of the lesson. Understanding exactly how to pace the lessons takes time. By paying attention to students' responses and rate of accuracy, you will gradually learn how to schedule the lessons so that students improve their reading and writing skills in a relaxed but efficient manner.

Preparing the Lessons

In preparing the lessons, develop the habit of following this procedure:

1. Familiarize yourself with the lesson students are to work on that day.

2. Review the appropriate lesson notes in Chapter 7 of this manual for suggestions to help you teach the lesson. Go over the appropriate answers in the Answer Key as well.

3. Review any notes you took after the preceding class in which you jotted down vocabulary words or writing difficulties that students need to review. Teacher note-taking is discussed in Chapter 6 of this manual.

4. Decide upon any reinforcement activities you may want to use and complete any preparation needed. Suggestions for reinforcement activities are given in Chapter 4.

5. Skim the lesson to be assigned for homework and the appropriate lesson notes so you can introduce the reading selection and answer any questions students may have about the exercises.

Last and most important, you need to prepare yourself mentally and emotionally for the class. If possible, take several minutes before the students' arrival to unwind from the previous activities of the day. As a general rule, how well the lesson goes is determined by how relaxed and focused you are on the work. As the teacher, your main function is to serve as a smooth bridge between the student and the lesson material. Your own patience and concentration will determine how helpful this "bridge" is.

The Teacher-Student Relationship

Making sure that you are relaxed for the lesson also contributes to the development of a good working relationship with your students. Adolescent or adult reading students rely heavily on your support and encouragement.

It is helpful to remember that most of us, as we grow older, learn to fake or avoid situations in which we feel inadequate. We prefer habits and routines that are familiar and give us some sense of security. Adolescent or adult reading students have entered into a situation in which they can neither avoid (unless they give up) or fake their way through the material. They are to be admired for having put themselves in this situation. Unless they are extremely motivated or thick-skinned, they must feel a sense of support from you or they will eventually drop out, because exposing their lack of knowledge just gets too painful after a while.

In addition, completing the lessons in these books *is* hard work. No matter how much progress is being made, virtually all students experience a sense of frustration at one time or another. Your encouragement will help them to get through these gloomy periods when they are ready to throw in the towel.

Suggestions for a Good Working Rapport

The following are suggestions to help you consider how best to develop a good working relationship with your students.

- Strive for naturalness in your voice and mannerisms. Some teachers unconsciously treat reading students as if they were mental invalids or victims of a ruthless society. A condescending or pitying approach does not help students become better readers.

- Greet the students pleasantly and spend a few minutes in casual conversation before you actually begin work. As a rule, do not allow this conversation to exceed five minutes. Students will take their cue from you. If you encourage conversing rather than working, they will be more than willing to oblige.

- Participate fully in this pre-lesson conversation and listen attentively to the students' remarks. Often you can later refer to these remarks when you are helping students to understand a vocabulary word or a point in the reading selection. Not only do they appreciate the fact that you actually were listening to them, but also they begin to make connections with the material they are studying.

- Use a phrase such as "Shall we get started?" to indicate that it is time to begin the lesson. A consistent use of such transitional statements helps the students feel more comfortable with both you and the class routine.

- If possible, work at an uncluttered table rather than at desks. Try to have straight-backed, cushioned chairs since physical comfort makes developing a good relationship easier.

- Be sure to use positive reinforcement during the lesson. Remind students of the progress they are making. When a student is particularly discouraged, do this in a concrete way. For example, show him how many pages of work he has completed, or have him look at his composition book to see all the writing he has done.

- Develop the habit of wishing students a good day or a good evening as they leave the class. This is especially important if both you and the students have had a rough session. The students, particularly adolescents, need to know that you don't carry personal grudges.

Classroom Supplies

For each class, students need to bring their *Challenger* book, their composition book, and a pen or pencil. The use of the composition book—a slim, loose-leaf binder with wide-lined paper—is discussed in Chapter 5.

You need your own copy of *Challenger*, any notes and reinforcement activities pertaining to the lesson, a few sheets of blank paper for notes, and a pen. A pen is recommended because students can spot your marginal notes and corrections more easily. Avoid red ink as it is frequently associated with too many bad memories.

Have a dictionary and, if possible, a set of encyclopedias, a globe or an atlas within easy reach. The encyclopedia and the dictionary are valuable resources because they provide pictures and additional information about many of the words, people, and events mentioned in the reading selections and exercises. Be prepared to teach students how to use these resources. Do not assume that students working at a Book 6 reading level are familiar with them.

A globe or map is helpful because it can make the facts presented in the lessons more meaningful to students. For example, in Lesson 2, Exercise 7 of Book 6, the students complete an exercise about state capitals. Many students don't know the location of many of the states mentioned in this exercise. This presents a good opportunity to locate the states on a map.

Encourage students to research additional information as often as their interest, abilities, and time permit and give them all the assistance you can when they need help. These mini-research experiences help students feel more competent when searching for information.

A Summary of Do's

1. Do try to schedule at least two classes each week which meet at a regularly-appointed time.
2. Do take time to develop a consistent lesson format that will work well for your students.
3. Do perceive your students' work in terms of improvement rather than mastery.
4. Do take time to prepare for each class.
5. Do give yourself a few moments to relax before each class.
6. Do develop a good working relationship with students because it is essential to their reading progress.
7. Do make sure that the environment in which you teach is as conducive to good learning as possible.
8. Do have reference and resource materials available, if possible.
9. Do give the students positive reinforcement during the lessons.

3. Teaching the Lessons

In this chapter, suggestions are given for teaching the main components of each lesson. These components include the word study, the reading selection, the exercises, correcting the homework, and the homework preview.

Word Study

The *Challenger* series places a great deal of emphasis on learning and/or reviewing word meanings since a major obstacle to reading development is a poor vocabulary. It has been estimated that only about 2,000 words account for 99% of everything we say. To be a proficient reader, however, one must be familiar with far more than 2,000 words. Thus, most of the exercises which follow each reading selection focus on vocabulary development.

Keep in mind that the *Challenger* series is a controlled vocabulary series. When students wish to know how the words listed in the Words for Study at the beginning of each lesson have been selected, inform them that these words are appearing for the first time in the series. Most of the other words in each lesson have appeared earlier in the series.

Students not only find the concept of a controlled vocabulary interesting, but some interpret this concept in interesting ways. For example, one student who was experiencing difficulty with a synonym exercise in Book 6 remarked: "Well, you can't expect me to know words that were studied in Book 5!"

Behind this statement is a conviction shared by many reading students that once you've studied a word, you should never have to study it again. Unfortunately, this is not true. Words are learned through repetition, practice, and using the dictionary. Do not assume that your students know this. Simply remind them, when appropriate, that a good reading vocabulary is necessary for good reading and that they will encounter a word in various types of exercises so that they can truly master its meaning.

The best way to encourage your students as they complete the many vocabulary development exercises is to demonstrate an interest in language yourself. This does not mean that you have to use a lot of "fancy" words when talking to your students. What it does mean is that you do not approach vocabulary study as if it were something to be merely endured.

Here are a few suggestions for making vocabulary study more interesting for students:

1. Have students pronounce the Words for Study in the next lesson during the homework preview. Most words will not give them any trouble. By pronouncing the unfamiliar ones, students will gain confidence in their ability to learn the word, and confidence often leads to interest.

2. Encourage students to develop the habit of paying attention to word endings. Words listed in the Words for Study appear in the same form in which they appear in the reading. For example, notice that in Book 6, Lesson 1, *measured* is listed. Emphasis on accurate pronunciations of endings will help students with both their reading and writing.

3. When time permits, spend a few minutes in casual conversation about some of the words. Using Book 6, Lesson 1 again as an example, you may wish to talk about two ways in which the word *stalk* can be used, or have students identify the root in *reality*, or help them trace the origin of *wallop* in a good dictionary. Occasional discussion of words helps students to see them as more than just a string of letters.

4. Take time during discussions of the readings to highlight vocabulary and/or language features. In Book 6, Lesson 1, students enjoy reading the opening dialogue aloud and acting out ways that people from other subcultures might express the same statements. These brief discussions help students to see that language patterns vary from group to group and that language is always changing.

5. Finally, strive to speak with expression. You needn't be a Broadway star, but a little ham goes a long way.

The Reading Selections

The amount of time you allot to oral reading and discussion of the reading selections ultimately depends on both the needs of your students and how much class time you have with them.

Oral Reading

Having students read aloud at least part of the reading selection periodically gives you an opportunity to note their strengths and weaknesses and also to help them develop good oral reading habits. Some students are under the impression that good oral reading means that one reads as fast as one can. Remind these students that in oral reading one must always be conscious of the needs of the listeners.

Discussing the Reading

Have a general discussion of the reading selection to refresh students' memories and to make sure they have understood the reading. Then discuss their responses to the comprehension exercises.

To create an atmosphere in which the reading selections and student thoughts about them can be discussed with a sense of harmony and unity, consider these suggestions.

1. Plan questions that you want to ask in class. Be prepared, however, to put your planned questions aside when a spontaneous question arises in class.

2. Make sure students understand the basic ground rule of all good discussions: one person speaks at a time.

3. Encourage participation, but don't force it. Likewise, discourage students from monopolizing the discussion.

4. Keep the discussion focused.

5. Avoid asking "yes" and "no" questions. Discussions, like travel, should be broadening. "Yes" and "no" questions shut off discussion by being answerable in a single word. They also imply that the student should have reached a conclusion before the discussion has even started.

6. If students seem confused by your questions, rephrase them rather than repeating them word-for-word. This practice is not only courteous, but it also reminds students that there is usually more than one way to phrase an idea.

These suggestions represent the easier part of moderating a discussion. The harder part is staying out of the way. Your task as the moderator is to get students to react to each other's opinions and comments, not to dominate the discussion yourself.

It is essential to view discussions in the same way that you view the students' other work—in terms of improvement, or growth, instead of mastery. It takes time to develop a good discussion group in which participants can learn to really listen to each other and gain confidence to express themselves as genuinely as possible. Do not expect it to be otherwise.

Through these discussions, students begin to sense a relationship between the lesson material and their own lives. The relationships they have with you and the other students can become more relaxed and real. This, in turn, means that everyone learns better and faster.

The Exercises

In the exercises, students develop their reasoning abilities because they are required to think and infer, to use context clues, to practice the process of elimination, and to apply what they already know to new situations.

Three points that you should emphasize to students are accuracy, legibility, and completeness. They are to spell their responses correctly and legibly, and they are not to leave any item blank. Tell them to answer all questions to the best of their ability. Not only does learning thrive on corrected mistakes, but also much is to be said for the art of intelligent guessing.

Remind students to check over their homework after they have finished all the exercises to make sure they have answered all questions completely and accurately.

Allow enough time at the end of the class period for previewing the exercises that are to be completed for homework. It is important that students understand exactly what is expected of them, so don't rush this segment of the lesson.

You should spend a few minutes during the first class meeting with your students to review the importance of homework. Remember, some of your students haven't been in a school situation for quite a while, and they may need to be reminded of the importance of completing the assignments as well as they can.

Sometimes students try to complete the homework right after a full day's (or full night's) work, or just before going to bed, or while they are trying to fulfill other responsibilities. Suggest that they schedule a definite, 30-minute study time in quiet surroundings when they are not exhausted.

Make sure to present your ideas on how to develop better study habits in the form of suggestions. You are not stating policy; you are simply encouraging students to think about how they can better achieve their reading goals within the circumstances of their lives.

Correcting the Homework

Be sure you allow enough time to go over the homework with the students. You will probably need to observe your students and try out a few different schedules before you hit on the pace that works best for them. But once you establish the appropriate pace, consistency promotes good concentration and effective learning.

Of all the lesson segments—the words for study, the reading selection, and the exercises—the exercises should be covered most thoroughly. All the homework should be corrected. Remember that many patterns are being established. If students develop the habit of doing something incorrectly, they will have a hard time unlearning the procedure. Be sure to explain this to the students. Eventually, they adapt to this procedure because they see that the more they correct in the early stages, the less they have to correct later.

Too often, going over the homework can be nothing more than a dry, mechanical routine in which students simply read their answers. Not only does this deprive them of practice with the words and concepts they've been studying, but also it is unfair. Consciously or unconsciously, the students' efforts are being slighted if the homework critique is being done in a dreary, "what's-the-answer-to-number-2?" style.

Take your time and enjoy this part of the lesson. If opportunities arise for brief tangents in which items are related to life experiences or other bits of information, take advantage of them.

Above all, don't forget to express your appreciation for students' efforts. Your supportive remarks should be brief and spoken in a natural voice. Excessive praise is ultimately as counterproductive as no praise at all. Words of encouragement should stress the notion of progress because students are progressing as they complete each lesson.

The Homework Preview

During the homework preview the students note what to do in the next lesson, which they are to complete for homework. Begin by going over the words listed in the Words for Study. Then introduce the reading selection to give students an idea of what they will be reading about. It may be necessary to help students get into the habit of noting the title of the reading selection. They should understand that the title gives them a general idea of what the selection is about and helps to focus their attention.

Remind students to refer to the reading selection when they cannot recall an answer to a comprehension question. In many instances, they may need to make intelligent guesses based on information which is implied rather than stated directly.

At this point in their reading development, all students are able to skim through the exercises and ask questions about words and/or directions with no assistance from you. The individual lesson notes indicate those instances in which you may want to emphasize certain words or directions.

A Summary of Do's

1. Do take time when necessary to explain to students how vocabulary study, the reading selections, and exercises contribute to their reading development.

2. Do make vocabulary study as interesting as possible.

3. Do encourage students to have an attitude of growth rather than fixed opinions in their discussions.

4. Do remind students, when necessary, of the significant role that homework plays in reading development.

5. Do emphasize the need for thoroughness, correct spelling, and accuracy in completing each exercise.

6. Do strive for completeness and enthusiasm in the homework reviews.

7. Do support the students' progress by taking the time to point out growth they have demonstrated in their work.

8. Do allow enough time at the end of each lesson to go over the Words for Study, introduce the next reading selection, and preview the homework exercises.

4. Reinforcement Activities

As the term suggests, these activities are designed to reinforce the students' understanding and retention of the lesson material. All students and most teachers occasionally need a break in the routine. Reinforcement activities may throw your schedule off a bit, but it's worth it. Just make sure that you leave enough time at the end of the class period to preview the homework.

At this point in students' development, two types of activities are particularly helpful:

- Activities which reinforce vocabulary skills.
- Occasional, short exercises which focus on mechanical or usage errors most of your students repeatedly make in their compositions.

The types of activities you use and the frequency with which you use them depend on the needs of your students and how often you have an opportunity to meet with them. The suggestions in this section are based on activities that students have found both helpful and enjoyable. This list is by no means complete. Take some time to develop your own "bag of tricks." Through talking with other teachers, skimming puzzle magazines, and using your own imagination, you will soon have reinforcement activities for a variety of skills. Students, too, often recall helpful activities from their earlier schooling. In fact, some of the suggestions which follow come from students.

Word and Information Games

Students working at this level often enjoy games that are modeled after television shows such as *Jeopardy*. These activities take some time to prepare, but they are an excellent way to reinforce vocabulary and information presented in the lessons. Certainly you can prepare the questions, but having the students do it gives them an excellent opportunity to review the material.

Students can create their own *Jeopardy* games by preparing sets of questions based on the reading selections. They can also create sets of vocabulary questions. For example, all the answers in a category might begin with the prefix *pre-* or the letter *s*. Other appropriate categories include: State Capitals, Bodies of Water, U.S. Presidents, Roman Gods and Goddesses, Famous Inventors, Abbreviations, and so on.

Other game show formats can also be used. For example, students enjoy playing their own version of *Wheel of Fortune*. They also enjoy their version of *College Bowl* in which two teams compete against each other. In this game, the teacher can prepare the questions and act as the moderator.

Puzzles

Many puzzles and other activities can be found in puzzle magazines sold in most drugstores and supermarkets. You can create your own puzzles using these formats and vocabulary from past and current word indexes. The word indexes for Book 6 are at the back of this manual. If you have access to a computer, there is software available for creating crossword puzzles into which you can insert vocabulary words to be reinforced.

Spelling Bees or Drills

This activity is most helpful when a specific principle is emphasized; for example, selecting words which all contain a specific suffix or consonant blend, or which belong to the same word family. Again, the word indexes at the back of this manual can be helpful in developing these activities. Drills should be spontaneous, brief—10 words is usually sufficient—and informally presented. In other words, they should not resemble a quiz in which students demonstrate mastery. Rather they are an opportunity to help students to better understand certain language principles that are giving them difficulty.

Worksheets

One type of worksheet can focus on some principle that is giving students trouble, such as recognizing analogies, using context clues, or making inferences. A popular type of worksheet for context clue or vocabulary reinforcement is to collect sentences from a newspaper or magazine in which troublesome words you have been working with appear. Set them up in a fill-in-the-blank format for the students to complete as a group. As one student once remarked, "You mean people actually *do* use these words?" You might also tell students to be on the lookout for these words and have them bring to class examples that they find in their own reading.

Another type of worksheet can give students practice with some aspect of writing, such as capitalization or punctuation. For example, many students neglect to use commas after introductory clauses. You might prepare ten sentences which begin with introductory clauses and have the students insert commas appropriately. Students find this type of introduction to grammar both tolerable and beneficial because it helps them to recall a rule they need for their own writing.

Enrichment Projects

Students can spend some time in the library seeking additional information about people or topics presented in the lessons and informally report their findings to the class. These reports can be given during the time set aside for reinforcement activities.

Any additional information that you can present also heightens the students' interest in the material. For example, for Unit 1 in Book 6, some pictures of the ornate movie theaters built in the 1920s can stimulate a lively discussion of movies and their impact on our culture. Other enrichment ideas are suggested in the individual lesson notes.

Activities Based on Student Needs

Occasionally students may have specific personal needs, such as filling out an application form or creating a resume, that can be fit comfortably into the lesson format as reinforcement activities if they tell you about them far enough in advance. However, reinforcement activities are to reinforce, not replace, the lessons. If students are spending most of their valuable class time hearing additional information about the reading selections or getting your assistance with personal needs, they may learn some interesting facts or get forms filled out, but they are not progressing in their reading development.

If you suspect that students are using reinforcement activities to avoid working on the lessons, you probably need to help them clarify their learning goals. Gently but firmly remind them that, in the long run, their reading and writing will progress more rapidly if they concentrate more on the lesson work and recognize that the primary reason for reinforcement activities is to do just that— reinforce.

A Note to the Teacher

Because it takes time to prepare many of these reinforcement activities, be sure to file them away for use with future students.

Also, do not pressure yourself to come up with something new every time you plan a reinforcement activity. It takes a few years to develop a solid file of activities.

A Summary of Do's and Don'ts

1. Do make sure the scheduled lesson time is not sacrificed for reinforcement activities.

2. Do involve the students in planning and creating reinforcement activities whenever possible.

3. Do plan and implement activities that address both the students' learning needs and their personal needs.

4. Do remember to save materials you develop for future use.

5. Don't foster a "here's-some-more-hard-work" attitude toward reinforcement activities. The students have just finished discussing a reading selection, reviewing their homework, and learning new material. If the reinforcement activities are to benefit them, they need a little more informality from you for this segment of the lesson.

6. Don't foster a "this-is-just-for-fun" attitude either. Students might not find the activities enjoyable. And you want students who do find them enjoyable to recognize that pleasure and learning can go hand in hand.

5. Writing

Because the major purpose of this reading series is to help students develop their reading skills, less emphasis has been placed on writing skills. Even though writing is an important skill, it is a distinct skill that requires a great deal of practice and instruction time. Generally, the writing activities included in Book 6 focus on clarity and completeness of expression, coherence of thought, basic grammar, and spelling. However, there are plentiful opportunities for students to express their own opinions and ideas in writing.

Why Writing Is Included

The teacher can assume that a student who has completed some of the books which precede Book 6 can write complete sentences and coherent paragraphs. These students will not be surprised at the exercises which involve writing in the later *Challenger* books.

Students who are new to this series may wonder why writing activities have been included in a reading series. When this is the case, take time to point out the following:

- Writing is part of literacy. To be literate, a person must be able to write as well as read.

- Writing helps students to formulate and express their thoughts more precisely. This type of thinking helps them to complete the other exercises more rapidly.

- The writing that students do in these lessons will help them with other types of writing they may want to do, such as letters, reports, and short paragraphs on job applications or resumes.

- Only through actually writing can students see that they are able to write.

Opportunities for Writing

In Book 6, an increasing emphasis is placed on content, rather than on the mechanics of writing. The reading comprehension questions require students to draw conclusions from inferences, to cite reasons to support their opinions, to give explanations for their answers, and to cite examples and details to support their responses. Exercises that focus on developing critical thinking include writing positive and negative statements, writing statements of fact and opinion, and interpreting poetry and cartoons. There are also opportunities for imaginative writing, including writing the endings to excerpts from longer works and writing descriptions of life in a different time or place.

The individual lesson notes include many suggestions for writing assignments which can supplement the lessons as reinforcement activities. As stated in Chapter 1, it is recommended that weekly writing assignments of 150-300 words be given. However, the decision on how often to give writing assignments as homework should depend on the teacher's assessment of the students' time, personal needs, and capabilities. The key word is flexibility.

How to Handle Writing Assignments

When students have been given a writing assignment, have them share their work at the beginning of the next class session. Working in pairs or small groups, students can read their assignments aloud to one another and react to each other's writing on the basis of content and organization. Students can then exchange papers and act as editors or proofreaders, checking for mechanical problems such as missing words, spelling, capitalization, and punctuation. Give students the opportunity to revise their assignments before collecting them at the following class session.

When responding to these writing assignments, try to make positive comments as well as noting areas for improvement. Your reactions should be based more on the content, style, and organization of the writing than on the mechanical aspects.

It is recommended that students keep all writing assignments in a slim, loose-leaf binder with wide-lined notebook paper. Composition books enable both the students and the teacher to quickly review student progress. Have them date their work. As the weeks and months progress, most students enjoy looking back now and then at all the writing they have done and how much they have accomplished.

Like reading and vocabulary work, writing must be seen in terms of improvement rather than mastery. Most students read far better than they write. It is not uncommon for a student working in Book 6, for example, to write at a Book 4 level: very simple sentences, few modifiers, and underdeveloped thoughts. The most common reason for this is lack of practice. Allow students to develop from their own starting points, making them aware of their strengths as well as helping them to work on their weaknesses. And don't forget to be patient.

Here are a few suggestions to consider in helping students with their writing:

- As often as possible, have students read their written responses or compositions aloud. Students usually enjoy doing this, and it gives them a chance to hear whether or not their writing makes sense. Insist on honest but courteously presented reactions from the other students.

- Occasionally, allot some class time to studying how the professional writers write. Use a reading selection from *Challenger* or an interesting magazine article. Help students analyze the piece of writing on the basis of content organization and style. Make sure students understand that the writing they are analyzing is more than a second, third, or fourth draft. Few students recognize the contribution editing makes in the writing process, and understanding this makes them feel less discouraged about their writing difficulties.

- With their permission, use writing from previous or present students as models to explain a particularly difficult writing assignment. Seeing the work of their peers often helps students realize that the teacher is not asking them to do the impossible.
- With their permission, compile a worksheet using sentences from student work which illustrate common mistakes. For example, a worksheet comprised of student-created run-on sentences is an excellent reinforcement activity. Students can work together in class to correct the errors and better understand how to avoid this particular writing problem.
- Provide the opportunity for students to publicly display their final drafts so other students can read them.

Dealing with Typical Writing Problems
Run-on Sentences

This situation demands consummate tact on your part because, invariably, the student thinks he has written a terrific sentence and is dismayed to learn that he has to divide it into three or four shorter sentences. Help him to see that, by using commas and periods wherever necessary, he helps readers to follow his thoughts more easily. To illustrate how punctuation helps the reader, have him read the sentence aloud, telling him to pause only at commas and to take a breath only at a period. If you prefer, you can demonstrate by reading his sentence to him. When he recognizes the value of punctuation marks, have him revise the run-on sentence as necessary. Be sure to commend him for his effort in helping to make his writing easier for readers to comprehend.

Omitted Words

When reading their sentences aloud, students are often surprised to see that they have omitted words. Remind them that many writers have this problem because the mind can think faster than the hand can write. Suggest that after they have written something, they should read it to themselves, pointing to each word as they encounter it. This strategy will help them learn to monitor their writing.

Confusing Sentences

When a student writes a sentence which is confusing, tell him you don't understand what he's trying to express and ask him to explain what he meant. Once you understand his intent, start a more coherent version of his sentence and have him finish it. After the student has read the revision, ask him if it matches what he meant. If not,

work on the sentence until the revision accurately expresses the student's original idea.

Problems with Content and Organization

Students often have difficulty finding enough to say in their writing assignments and organizing their thoughts in a logical or interesting manner. Suggest that they begin by making notes of everything they can think of pertaining to the topic. The next step is to select from their notes the specific points and details that they want to include in their composition. Then they should organize those points and details in the order in which they want to include them. They should do all of this *before* writing their first draft. After the first draft is written, they should read it to see if they want to add anything more or to rearrange any of the points.

A Summary of Do's and Don'ts

1. Do tailor writing assignments to meet the students' needs and capabilities.
2. Do make sure that students understand the purpose and value of writing practice.
3. Do have students keep an orderly composition book for all their writing.
4. Do make sure that written work is evaluated, and when appropriate, have students write at least a second draft.
5. Do provide opportunities for students to share their writing with each other.
6. Don't expect the students' writing levels to be as high as their reading levels.
7. Don't allow writing assignments to become more important than the lessons and other necessary reinforcement activities.

6. Using the Lesson Notes

Because you are already familiar with the principles and procedures that pertain to the lessons in general from reading the previous chapters in this manual, you have the necessary foundation for sound instructional practices. The lesson notes address some specific points for the individual lessons. As part of class preparation, you should review the notes for the lesson assigned for homework. You should also read the notes for the lesson which you will be previewing to decide on how best to introduce the reading and to note any suggestions and reminders that might be helpful to the students when they are doing their homework.

Keep in mind that the lesson notes are only suggestions based on the experience of other reading teachers. If you try one of the suggestions a few times and find it doesn't work, disregard it.

Items of Primary and Secondary Emphasis

In most cases, the items listed under the "Primary emphasis" heading deal with reading comprehension, forming and writing reasoned opinions, and using context clues. Reading comprehension always receives primary emphasis because students are applying what they are learning to all parts of the lesson. The first time a particular task is introduced as an exercise, it also is listed under "Primary emphasis."

Items listed under "Secondary emphasis" receive less emphasis in the lesson. Many are skills which have been introduced previously and are now being reinforced. Occasionally, an item normally receiving secondary emphasis, such as analogies, is listed under "Primary emphasis" because more emphasis than usual has been given to a particular skill in order to review and assess the students' progress.

The Reading Selection

The lesson notes contain suggestions for introducing the reading selections and for discussing them. The reading segment of the lesson demands more flexibility on the teacher's part than any other. Students vary greatly in ability and motivation. Remember that the key to helping students make the greatest gains in the least amount of time is observation. Carefully monitoring your students' progress will help you to develop sound procedures for improving reading and comprehension skills.

Developing Your Own Notes

Develop the habit of keeping your own notes. Take time at the end of each class session to write down any remarks or reminders about particular difficulties students may have had with the lesson. Also make note of specific words or skills for which you may want to develop reinforcement activities.

Also, be sure to keep notes of any procedures and techniques which seem to work well. Often you will hit upon an excellent way to present a certain skill or concept. Take some time to jot down your idea, especially if you know that you won't have the opportunity to use it again until a much later time. So much patience and concentration is called for in teaching reading that it's easy to forget those great ideas.

7. Lesson Notes for Book 6

Lesson 1

It Don't Hurt Much, Ma'am

Primary emphasis

- Reading comprehension (nonfiction)
- Using context clues
- Forming a reasoned opinion

Secondary emphasis

- Vocabulary review (Which Word Does Not Fit?)
- The suffix -ment
- Forming the plural of words ending with f and fe

Words for Study

The Words for Study section includes words that appear in this lesson which have not been introduced previously in this controlled vocabulary reading series.

Have the students pronounce the new words prior to reading the selection. Generally, students should have difficulty with no more than five of these words. When a student does have trouble sounding out a new word, remind him of appropriate phonics and syllabication rules he can use so that he does the sounding out rather than you. For some words, guide words provide helpful cues. For example, one student found that by jotting *California* above *caliber,* he could immediately recall the correct pronunciation of *caliber.* After students have pronounced the new words, have them briefly review those words with which they had difficulty.

This type of pronunciation drill is most helpful for students who have completed at least three of the preceding books in this series. Remember, this is a new book, and many students experience some degree of stage fright when beginning a new book. By having students sound out the new words and by briefly reviewing troublesome ones, you help them to see that they indeed have the skills to work in Book 6.

For some students, particularly those who scored approximately 6.0 on word recognition tests and/or are beginning in this book, it is more expedient to correct any mispronunciations by simply saying the word correctly. The primary benefit of Book 6 for these students is that it offers an opportunity to improve skills in studying, comprehension, reasoning, writing, and vocabulary. A phonics approach to troublesome words is unnecessary for these students, and it also often turns them right off.

Think of these students as you think of yourself. For example, if you ask a person for the correct pronunciation of *Jacuzzi,* you don't need to hear that the *c* is hard, the *u* has a long *oo* sound, the *i* has a long *e* sound, and the accent is on the second syllable. You simply need to hear the word and perhaps repeat it a few times. Phonics rules are like the safety ropes in a swimming pool. You only heed their presence when you need the security they offer.

There are exceptions to this rule, of course. For example, some Book 6 students consistently neglect certain word endings or confuse *per-* with *pre-.* In these cases, emphasize the trouble spot by having the student sound out the word rather than merely saying it correctly for him.

As was the case with the preceding books in this series, most of the new words appear in subsequent reading selections and exercises so that students have many opportunities to work with them. Thus, there is no need to strive for immediate mastery; mastery will come with practice.

This principle also holds true for word definitions. Students should not be expected to have mastered the meanings of the new words by the end of the lesson in which they first appear. Generally, when students ask for the meaning of a Word for Study that they are sounding out, a simple statement such as, "See if you can figure it out when you come to it in the lesson," is helpful.

Times occur, however, when it is helpful to give an on-the-spot definition, sentence, or example of an unfamiliar word. Perhaps a student needs to know that he has a working relationship with you. Perhaps he has had a difficult day and needs a few moments to center himself on the work. Whatever the reason, a few seconds of friendly conversation is more important than reminding him of the value of context clues.

Make your responses lighthearted and interesting. For example, a student, after having sounded out the word *gallop,* wanted to know what it meant. Knowing that the student never had a chance to eat dinner until after class, the teacher responded, "Louise was so hungry when she got home from night school that she galloped to the refrigerator as if she were a horse."

Reading Selection

Tell students that the reading selections which appear in Book 6 have been adapted from the works of professional writers. It motivates students to know that they are reading material that has enjoyed critical acclaim and has been written for the general adult reading public.

Introduce the reading selection by briefly discussing movie and TV westerns. Tell students that the reading discusses some of the differences between how movies and TV depict the Old West and what it was really like.

Generally, all initial readings of the selections should be done for homework. However, because this is the first lesson, allot time for an oral first reading in class. This gives you an opportunity to assess the strengths and weaknesses of students' oral reading abilities. Begin by reading the first part of the story yourself, and then ask for volunteers to continue.

Because Book 6 contains both fiction and nonfiction reading selections, it is important to introduce or review these terms for the students. Lesson 1 offers an excellent opportunity for this because both fiction and nonfiction are included in the reading passage. The best time to discuss these concepts is after the students have completed the reading. Point out the introductory material set in italics and ask them how this part differs from the rest of the selection.

After reading the selection aloud, discuss it in a general way. This gives students a chance to get a sense of the selection as a whole while giving you the opportunity to assess their comprehension skills.

When you have completed the general discussion of the reading selection, preview the exercises to be done for homework. Since this is the first lesson, take plenty of time and be sure all students understand how to do each exercise. If necessary, have students complete an item in each exercise so that they have a thorough understanding of how to do the work.

Exercise 1: About the Reading

During the homework preview, have the students read the directions and remind them that they are to refer to the reading selection for any answer they cannot recall. Students need to know that having to refer to the reading selection for the correct answer does *not* mean they are poor readers. Tell students who suffer from this false impression that instead it means that they are good students!

During the homework preview, you also want to encourage students to write a well-developed answer for the "What do you think?" question. Many students find the instruction, "Use all the lines to write your answer," helpful. The goal is not wordiness; the goal is learning to support one's opinions and thoughts with sound reasons. Because this type of question appears frequently in Book 6, plan to spend quite a bit of time discussing the strengths and weaknesses of the students' writing during the homework review.

All writing mistakes should be corrected—preferably by the students with your assistance. There is no need to explain the rule for every correction. By noting the corrections, however, students gradually become accustomed to standard writing procedures. Their writing will improve, and it will become much easier.

Exercise 2: Which Word Does Not Fit?

During the homework preview, encourage students to use a dictionary for any words they do not know. All answers should be spelled accurately.

Exercise 3: Words That End with -*ment*

During the homework preview, remind the students that they need not complete the sentences in the order in which they appear. If necessary, teach them how to use the process of elimination to complete this exercise.

Many students find it helpful if you remind them to read each sentence in its entirety prior to filling in the blanks. For example, sentence 2 should be read "Al ordered an *blank*-ment of his girlfriend's photograph for his desk at work."

For any incorrect answers, help students to identify context clues during the homework review. Granted this is time-consuming, but because this is the first lesson, you want to initiate good working patterns. All words should be spelled accurately.

Exercise 4: Who Was Wild Bill Hickok?

During the homework preview, tell students to read each entire sentence before attempting to find the correct answer. Tell them to pay attention to word endings and context clues in deciding which word to place in each blank. Also, they should not feel they must complete the sentences in the order in which they appear. If necessary, remind them that checking off words after they have used them is a helpful practice.

When students have finished filling in the blanks, have them read the entire passage again for comprehension.

During the homework review, discuss how suffixes provide important clues in identifying the correct answer.

Exercise 5: Spelling

If necessary, review the meanings of *singular* and *plural*.

Notes

1. After the students—especially any new students—have gone over the exercises and made any necessary corrections during the homework review, give them an opportunity to ask questions or make comments about what they have just accomplished. If they seem overwhelmed by the work, point out the strengths they have shown in completing the work. Remind them that this is only the first lesson and that they will get used to the work more quickly than they think possible.

2. A follow-up activity is not recommended for the first lesson. After all, enough is enough! If one seems appropriate, however, consider having your students watch a television program and jot down four or five examples of violence. Dialogue and commercials are to be included in their critique. Discussion about this activity is more interesting when everyone has agreed to watch the same program. Strive to help students clarify their own definitions of violence rather than presenting them with a pat description.

Lesson 2

Will Rogers

Primary emphasis

- Reading comprehension (autobiography)
- Forming a reasoned opinion
- Vocabulary development

Secondary emphasis

- The suffix -ment
- Using context clues
- Using reference materials

Words for Study

Use the procedure suggested for Lesson 1.

Reading Selection

During the homework preview, review the meaning of *autobiography* and *biography*. Point out the two sets of asterisks separating the three parts of this reading. Tell students that one part is biographical and two parts are autobiographical.

For the discussion of the reading, try to have *The Will Rogers Scrapbook* available for students to look at. It has terrific pictures.

Exercise 1: About the Reading

Remind students to read the selection carefully *prior* to answering the comprehension questions. Not only will their reading improve, but also they will find Book 6 far more enjoyable.

The answer for question 10 cannot be found in the reading selection. Mention this during the homework preview and tell students to make an "intelligent guess."

Exercise 2: Arithmetic Problem

If necessary, define the word *arithmetic* during the homework preview. Many students are not familiar with this word. If students have difficulty getting started, discuss the process of subtracting the year Will Rogers was born from the year he died.

Exercise 3: What Do You Think?

Remind students that for What Do You Think? questions, they are to respond with their own opinions in good sentence form. There is no one right answer. However, they are to support their opinions with sound reasons. A suggested follow-up writing activity topic is "What Kind of Movie Star Will Be Popular in My Grandchild's Time?"

Exercise 4: Pleasure

Remind the students to use the process of elimination to complete this exercise and to check off their choices as they make them.

Exercise 5: Displeasure

In addition to the process of elimination, some students may find a dictionary helpful for this exercise. Many of these words have been selected because they gave students working in Book 5 difficulty.

Exercise 6: More Work with the Ending -ment

During the homework preview, remind the students to read the complete sentence and to use context clues as a guide to putting the right word in each sentence. Remind them also that they need not complete the sentences in the order in which they appear. During the review, be sure they have capitalized *Detachment* in number 9.

Exercise 7: The Capitol and Capitals

Tell the students to use a dictionary for any capitals they do not know. Many students are not aware of the fact that the dictionary gives this kind of information. If students ask whether they should look up the city or the state, suggest that they try both ways and see what happens.

During the homework review, review the difference between *Capitol* and *capital*. Make sure students have capitalized the capitals. Because capitalization is stressed in subsequent lessons, the more practice students have, the better. Students enjoy having a map of the U.S. available so they can locate the capitals as they match them with their respective states.

Lesson 3

Some Facts about Motion Pictures

Primary emphasis

- Reading comprehension (nonfiction)
- Vocabulary (synonyms and antonyms)
- Using context clues

Secondary emphasis

- The suffix -ness
- Capitalization
- Spelling (changing the *y* to *i*)

Words for Study

For some students, a brief discussion of the definitions for *persistence* and *image* are helpful prior to their reading the selection.

When they are saying the new words, have students give both pronunciations for *separate*, with and without the stress on the final syllable.

Reading Selection

Since motion pictures are familiar to most people, the reading selection can be introduced in a number of ways. You might briefly discuss silent movies students have seen, or find out if any have taken home movies. Allot some time during the homework review to discuss *persistence of vision*.

Exercise 1: About the Reading

Most students answer question 12 correctly, but they are still not certain what *plot* means. Briefly discuss this term with them during the review.

Exercise 2: Synonyms

Remind students to use the dictionary for unfamiliar words and to use the process of elimination.

Exercise 3: Antonyms

Students are to use the same procedure as they did to complete Exercise 2. Review the terms *synonym* and *antonym* during the homework review.

Exercise 4: Spelling

Students should have no trouble completing this exercise accurately.

Exercise 5: Words That End with *-ness*

If necessary, remind students to use context clues and the process of elimination. They need not complete the sentences in order. As is the case with all exercises—especially when there is copying involved—accurate spelling should be emphasized.

Exercise 6: Capitalization Rules: Part 1

During the homework preview, go over each rule and the examples. Remind students to refer to the rules if necessary while completing the exercise. Point out in the exercise that the number in parentheses at the end of each sentence indicates how many words need to be capitalized. Review the rules during the homework review. More rules are presented in subsequent lessons and if students have a good understanding of these rules, they will find the future rules easier.

Lesson 4
We're the Only Colored People Here
Primary emphasis
- Comprehension of literature (short story)
- Forming a reasoned opinion
- Vocabulary (synonyms and antonyms)
- Using context clues

Secondary emphasis
- The suffix *-ness*
- Capitalization
- Spelling (changing the *y* to *i*)

Words for Study

Because *Colored* is in the title and *Negroes* is in the word list, some students may jump to the conclusion that the story is racist. It is preferable to suggest that students not make up their minds until after they have read the story. However, if they insist on raising the issue, you can mention that Gwendolyn Brooks is black, and, if necessary, point out the copyright date of 1953. In this case, a good follow-up discussion topic or writing assignment is "What Kind of Words Cause Me to Jump to Conclusions about People?"

Story

Review the meanings of *fiction* and *nonfiction* in introducing the story.

Students usually enjoy reading this story aloud. If time permits, have them do this during the homework review.

Exercise 1: About the Story

Both the content and form of the students' answers should be discussed carefully and courteously during the homework review. Responses to questions 7 and 8 usually vary greatly. Accept any response as long as students' reasons support their opinions. Question 9 can lead to a discussion of what changes, if any, have taken place since this story was written.

Exercise 2: Synonyms

Students are to use the same procedure as they did for Exercise 2 in Lesson 3.

Exercise 3: Antonyms

Students use the same procedure as they did for Exercise 3 in Lesson 3. If necessary, again review the definitions for *synonym* and *antonym*.

Exercise 4: More Work with the Ending *-ness*

Students use the same procedure as they did for previous exercises pertaining to suffixes.

Exercise 5: Spelling

If students have trouble remembering how they completed this work in the previous lesson, have them refer to that lesson rather than showing them how to change the *y* to *i*.

Exercise 6: Capitalization Rules: Part 2

As in Lesson 3, preview each rule and the examples. Then review the rules in Lesson 3. Remind students to refer to these rules if necessary while completing the exercise. Point out as before that the number in parentheses at the end of each sentence indicates how many words need to be capitalized. Allot time also for reviewing both these rules and the ones presented in Lesson 3 during the homework review.

In some editions, there is a misprint in question 6. *Jell-O* is a trademark and the *O* should be capitalized, as well as the *J*.

Lesson 5

Please Don't Shoot My Dog

Primary emphasis
- Reading comprehension (autobiography)
- Forming a reasoned opinion
- Using context clues

Secondary emphasis
- Vocabulary (compound words)
- Word families
- Capitalization

Reading Selection
During the homework preview, review the term *autobiography*. Ask the students which other lesson contained an example of autobiographical writing. (The answer is Lesson 2.) If possible, have pictures of Jackie Cooper as a child and as an adult actor to show the students.

Exercise 1: About the Reading
Encourage students to use all the lines that have been provided to develop their answers. As they are correcting any writing errors during the homework review, be sure to mention the improvement they are making. Have them compare the writing they did in Lesson 1 with their writing in Lesson 5.

What do you think?: Students usually want to know what actually happened. This is described in the Answer Key.

Exercise 2: Compound Words
Remind students to use a dictionary for any compound word they are not sure about.

Exercise 3: Word Families
Encourage students who have difficulty with this type of exercise to read each item aloud so they can hear which word should go where. Make sure students capitalize *Desperate* in number 7.

Exercise 4: Tears
Remind students that the process of elimination is a helpful strategy for completing this exercise. Encourage them to use context clues and word endings as guides. Remind them also to read the entire passage through after filling in the blanks.

Exercise 5: Capitalization Review
During the homework preview, remind students to refer to the rules they studied in Lessons 3 and 4 and to make sure they capitalize a total of 20 words.

Review: Lessons 1-5

It should be emphasized to the students that this is a review, not a test. These exercises are opportunities to review words and concepts that have been introduced in previous lessons. Material is often presented in new ways to both challenge students and arouse their interest. An overall score of 80% or better on a review exercise should be considered excellent.

Exercise 1: Word Review
For this and the other exercises, encourage students to refer to previous lessons or a dictionary for any words they cannot recall. Make sure they have spelled and capitalized words correctly.

Exercise 3: Suffixes
This is the first time the word *suffix* is formally introduced. Review the meaning of this word during the homework review. Have students identify the common suffixes in each set of answer choices.

Exercise 5: Review of Capitalization Rules
During the preview, review the ten rules that students studied in Lessons 3 and 4. If students have trouble thinking of examples, have them refer to these lessons for ideas, but insist that they come up with original examples.

Exercise 6: Compound Words
During the homework preview, go over the directions carefully with the students. Point out that they can work back and forth between the map clues and the definitions. For example, most students quickly see that the answers to questions 10 and 11 begin with an *h* and an *i* respectively. They can then put these two letters on the tenth and eleventh blanks next to the map (the two middle blanks to the right of the word *State*). With these clues, almost all students realize that the name of the state is *Ohio* and then know that answers 9 and 12 will each begin with an *o*.

If they wish, students may use the dictionary to help them solve the puzzle. But, as one student remarked, "What's the fun in solving a puzzle if you're going to use the dictionary?"

Lesson 6

Voices from the Great Depression

Primary emphasis
- Reading comprehension (nonfiction)
- Forming a reasoned opinion
- Vocabulary (synonyms)

Secondary emphasis
- Using context clues
- The suffix -ful
- The suffix -less
- A review of capitalization rules

Words for Study
If students are unfamiliar with *caseworker* and *psychiatrist*, you may want to spend some time briefly discussing these words during the preview.

Reading Selection
During the preview, briefly discuss the Great Depression so students will be aware of the conditions that are being described, and point out that Studs Terkel's book is a collection of first-person interviews. Many of the names in this reading are new words for students. If necessary, help the students to pronounce these names during the preview.

Exercise 1: About the Reading
After reviewing their answers to the questions, students may want to discuss the character or characters in the reading selection with whom they most sympathize.

Exercise 2: What Do You Think?
After the students have discussed their responses, it is helpful to provide some pictures of this period of American history. Many students are not familiar with the Great Depression, and pictures can help them better understand this era.

Exercise 4: The Suffix -ful
If necessary, remind students to use context clues and the process of elimination to help them choose the correct answers for this and the next exercise.

Exercise 6: Review of Capitalization Rules
During the homework preview, review the ten rules studied in Lessons 3 and 4 and remind students to check the number of words they capitalize in each sentence against the number in parentheses.

The Great Depression presents an opportunity for mini-research projects. Students who show an interest in this period can select a topic for further research and present either an oral or written report. Or a writing assignment on the topic "Lessons to Be Learned from the Great Depression" could be given.

Lesson 7

When John Quincy Adams Lost His Job

Primary emphasis
- Reading comprehension (biography)
- Identifying symbols
- Reading classified ads

Secondary emphasis
- Word families
- Forming a reasoned opinion
- Reasoning and spelling (Can You Crack the Code?)

Words for Study
Discuss the definition of the hyphenated prefix *ex-* if students are not familiar with its meaning.

Reading Selection
Review the terms *biography* and *autobiography* during the preview. Remind students that the readings in Lessons 2 and 5 were autobiographical, while this one is biographical.

Because it does not occur to many students that prominent figures in history suffer just like the rest of us mortals, this concept can be the basis for a good follow-up discussion topic.

Exercise 1: About the Reading
The answers to several of these questions are not specifically given in the reading selection but can be inferred from the information given. If students have trouble drawing the correct conclusions, discuss the process of inferring the best choice.

Exercise 2: Symbols
Review the definition of *symbol* during the homework preview. Remind students to use the process of elimination and intelligent guessing to complete the exercise. They may also want to ask a friend to help.

Exercise 3: Word Families
Remind students who have trouble with this type of exercise to complete it aloud so they can hear which word should go where.

Exercise 4: Looking for a Job
Many students wish to know if the advertisements in this exercise are examples of real ads. The answer is yes. Point out that in most newspapers ads are listed alphabetically by the first word.

Explain that some abbreviations, such as *bet.* and *exper.*, are not standard in other types of writing but are commonly used in classified ads.

Exercise 5: Can You Crack the Code?

Although these puzzles require quite a bit of work, students generally enjoy them. If necessary, help students get off to a good start by having them put *J*s above all the *B*s. Once they understand the procedure for cracking the code, they have little difficulty completing this exercise correctly. It will be easier for the students who notice that numbers 9 and 10 have the same first name as the example, and that 3, 4, and 7 also share a first name.

Lesson 8

Looking for a Job?
Primary emphasis

- Reading comprehension (nonfiction)
- Forming a reasoned opinion

Secondary emphasis

- Using context clues
- Forming compound words
- Vocabulary (antonyms)
- The suffix *-ly*
- Capitalization

Reading Selection

Introduce the reading by pointing out the italicized headings. Especially for adult students, the concept of "faulty thinking" is intriguing. Many students have never considered that there might be a "faulty" way to think about something.

Students often enjoy using the author's format to enumerate "faulty thinking" and successful "keys" for other areas of their lives, such as meeting new people, responding to authority, and handling rejection.

Exercise 1: About the Reading

During the preview, be sure students understand that their responses should reflect their understanding of the reading and not their own opinions. Because many students have their own pet theories about the job hunt, statements 5 and 7 agree with the author's point of view so that students have an opportunity to discriminate between what was stated in the passage and what wasn't.

Exercise 2: Jobs

Students are not familiar with many of the jobs described in this exercise. In addition to context clues, encourage them to use a dictionary by looking up the words in List A to see what compound words are formed from them.

Exercise 4: The Suffix *-ly*

It is not necessary to introduce the term *adverb* at this point. It is enough that students understand that the suffix *-ly* usually tells how something is done.

Exercise 6: Capitalization Rules: Part 3

As before, preview each rule and the examples and then review the rules learned in Lessons 3 and 4. Remind students to refer to all the rules if necessary when completing the exercise.

Exercise 7: A Skills Survey

Students invariably enjoy this exercise. In some instances, their responses to question 5 will contradict their responses to the previous questions. Use any contradictions as the basis for an interesting discussion. Corrections should be limited to errors in form rather than content.

As an additional writing activity, students can expand on this concept and write about the job they would most like to have. Have them describe the job and tell why they would like it.

Lesson 9

The Job Interview
Primary emphasis

- Reading comprehension (nonfiction)
- Classifying information
- Writing positive and negative responses
- Filling out an employment application

Secondary emphasis

- Using context clues
- Abbreviations
- The suffix *-ly*

Words for Study

Several of these new words are difficult. Take extra time when going over them, so that students will feel comfortable when they meet them in the lesson.

Reading Selection

Introduce this reading by briefly discussing job interview experiences students may have had. Point out that this reading selection is from the same source as the reading in Lesson 8.

A helpful follow-up activity to this lesson is to have interested students role-play a job interview. Role-playing is particularly useful in helping students to see that the job interview situation can be difficult for both the interviewer and the person being interviewed.

Exercise 1: About the Reading

Most students answer question 7 correctly but are not really certain what some of the other adages mean. Briefly discuss those which confuse students and have them cite examples that illustrate the validity of these sayings.

Exercise 2: Positive and Negative

Students enjoy reading these responses aloud. As a follow-up activity, have students choose which response they would probably make to each situation. They can then decide whether they have "positive" or "negative" outlooks.

Exercise 4: More Work with Classifications

Make sure students know what each abbreviation stands for, and check for proper capitalization and periods.

Exercise 6: Filling out an Employment Application

This exercise provides an excellent opportunity to remind students during the preview of the practical benefits of accurate spelling and legibility. Also remind them to read the statement directly above the signature line carefully. Review any words students are not sure of and the term *Equal Opportunity Employer*.

Because this exercise represents a real situation for many students, spend time carefully reviewing their responses during the homework review.

Lesson 10

How to Avoid a Job
Primary emphasis

- Comprehension of literature (fiction)
- Using context clues
- Analogies (word relationships)

Secondary emphasis

- A review of suffixes
- Spelling

Reading Selection

Introduce the selection by pointing out that this passage about whitewashing the fence is one of the best-known episodes in this popular work. Ask if students are already familiar with it. Review the meaning of fiction.

Exercise 1: About the Story

This reading selection and the comprehension questions should produce some lively discussion during the homework review. You might also want to discuss Twain's use of humor and compare it with Will Roger's writing in Lesson 2.

Exercise 3: Word Relationships

Students often have difficulty with this type of exercise. Help them get started by going over the first question during the preview. Ask them to explain the relationship between *image* and *sight*. Have them read the four choices and then decide which pair of words expresses a similar relationship. Most students will see that "food is to taste" has the same relationship as "image is to sight." If students are still confused, have them do the second one. Since *major* and *minor* are antonyms, this relationship is easier to recognize and verbalize.

Remind students that the process of elimination is often helpful in selecting the correct answer, and that they may use the dictionary to look up words they have forgotten. Whether or not you choose to introduce the term *analogy* is up to you. Some students are impressed by this word.

Exercise 4: Review of Suffixes

Go over the directions and example carefully during the homework preview. Be sure students understand that dropping the final *e* of *judge* before adding the suffix is an exception to the general rule. If necessary, remind the students of the spelling rule pertaining to changing the *y* to *i*.

Exercise 5: Spelling

Some students miss number 9 because they don't realize that a missing apostrophe constitutes a misspelled word. Remind them of this. Encourage students to use a dictionary when necessary.

For an additional writing activity, students could select one or more of these statements and explain the meaning in detail.

Exercise 6: What Exactly Is a Jew's Harp?

Remind students to read the entire passage through after they have filled in the blanks.

Review: Lessons 1-10

As with the review for Unit 1, remind students that this is not a test. These exercises are additional opportunities to review words and concepts that were introduced in previous lessons. Encourage students to refer to those lessons or to a dictionary for words they cannot recall. An overall score of 80% or better on a review exercise should be considered excellent.

Exercise 3: Compound Words

This exercise is a bit more difficult than previous exercises dealing with compound words. Remind students that they need not work in the order in which the sentences appear and that the process of elimination and a dictionary are helpful tools.

Exercise 4: Review of Capitalization Rules

By drawing attention to the example during the homework preview, most students soon realize that this exercise isn't nearly so difficult as it appears.

Exercise 5: Looking for a Job

During the preview, read aloud a few of these ads to be sure students can understand the unfamiliar abbreviations often found in classified ads. Remind them that these are often unorthodox abbreviations and are not acceptable in more formal writing.

The classified ads can be the basis of further discussion or composition topics. If students enjoyed role-playing an interview situation in Lesson 9, they may want to repeat that activity by selecting an ad and playing the roles of interviewer and applicant. Or they may select an ad and write a letter of application for the position.

Exercise 6: Find The Quote

Students who have worked in previous books in the *Challenger* series are familiar with this type of puzzle. Remind them to fill in the appropriate blanks for the quote as they answer each item. In this way, they can work back and forth between the clues and the quote, using context clues in the quote to complete partially filled-in words.

During the review, students enjoy swapping tricks they have developed to help them solve the puzzle. They also enjoy hearing any tricks you might have developed for problem-solving.

Lesson 11

Life on the Mississippi
Primary emphasis

- Reading comprehension (autobiography)
- Matching causes and effects
- Forming a reasoned opinion
- Using context clues

Secondary emphasis

- Vocabulary review (synonyms and antonyms)
- Reading a travel brochure
- Forming contractions

Words for Study

During the homework preview, make sure students understand the meanings of *accommodated* and *Jacuzzi*.

Reading Selection

Introduce the reading by pointing out that, like the selection in Lesson 10, this was also taken from a book by Mark Twain. Tell students that while *The Adventures of Tom Sawyer* is humorous fiction, *Life on the Mississippi* is autobiographical and this selection is not humorous.

Students usually enjoy reading this selection aloud during the homework review. Pictures of steamboats are helpful, since many students do not know what a steamboat is.

Exercise 1: About the Reading

During the preview, make sure students understand the concept of cause and effect.

Some students regard the "What do you think?" question as a good opportunity to discuss their own experiences with and attitudes about death; others have no inclination whatsoever to explore this topic. Use discretion in deciding whether or not to have students elaborate on this subject.

Exercise 2: Synonyms and Antonyms

A suggestion that is helpful for many students is to have them first correctly match all the synonyms and then tackle the antonyms.

Exercise 3: Idle Threats

By using the process of elimination, most students, even though they may not know the definitions for all the words, are able to complete this exercise with at least 80% accuracy, which is acceptable. It is not necessary to make sure students know the meanings of all unfamiliar words, since they appear in subsequent lessons. Of course, if students ask for specific definitions, by all means help them to understand what the words mean.

Exercise 4: Contractions

During the homework review, make sure students understand the meaning of *contraction*. If necessary, review the term *apostrophe*.

Exercise 5: Traveling by Steamboat

A good follow-up discussion or writing topic for question 10 is "My Idea of the Perfect Vacation."

Lesson 12

The Automobile Revolution
Primary emphasis

- Reading comprehension (nonfiction)
- Forming a reasoned opinion
- Using context clues

Secondary emphasis

- Analogies (word relationships)
- The prefix *un-*
- Forming contractions
- Taking a written driver's test

Words for Study

Many students associate the word *revolution* with warfare. Make sure they understand *revolution* also means "any extremely important change in a situation." Also, make sure students understand *mph* and *yield*.

Reading Selection

Use the concept of revolution as change to introduce the reading selection. After students have read the selection, discuss why the automobile did create a "revolution."

An activity which helps students to understand this more clearly is to have them list as many features of their hometown as they can think of which would not be there if it weren't for the automobile. Or you might have them list as many words as they can think of that wouldn't be in our vocabulary if it weren't for the automobile.

Exercise 2: What Do You Think?

A good follow-up writing activity topic is: "Describe the changes that would occur if your idea of the most popular form of travel 100 years from now actually happened."

Exercise 3: Word Relationships

If students still have difficulty with analogies, go over the first question during the homework preview. Remind students that the process of elimination is a helpful strategy.

Exercise 4: The Prefix *un-*

During the homework review, make sure students have capitalized *Unsafe* in number 10.

Exercise 5: More Work with Contractions

If necessary, review the term *contraction*. Also, make sure students are placing their apostrophes correctly.

Exercise 6: Taking a Written Driver's Test

Students who drive may want to discuss their own experiences in taking their driver's tests.

Lesson 13
Caught in Traffic
Primary emphasis

- Comprehension of literature (short story and poem)
- Forming a reasoned opinion
- Using context clues

Secondary emphasis

- Interpreting adages
- Prefixes that mean *not*
- Forming the singular possessive

Words for Study

Save any discussion of *Cupid*, *mythology*, and *Apollo* for the homework review. Some of the questions about these words are answered in Exercise 3.

Reading Selection

In introducing this story, mention that O. Henry is famous for his surprise endings. During the discussion, have the students state the surprise ending of this story. Ask students when they think this story took place, and discuss the clues on which they base their opinions.

Exercise 2: More Prefixes That Mean *Not*

During the review, be sure students have capitalized *Improper*, *Indecent*, and *Nonsense* in numbers 10, 11, and 13.

Exercise 3: A Fat Boy without Any Clothes On

Remind students to read the entire passage after filling in the blanks.

You might bring in several pictures of Cupid. (Traditional Valentine's cards are a good source.) Most students will recognize him readily.

If students seem particularly interested in this Greek myth, you might consider bringing in other myths for them to read.

Exercise 4: The Apostrophe to Show Ownership

This is the first of several exercises on using the apostrophe to show ownership. Go over the examples carefully during the preview. Be sure students recognize the signal word *of* and point out the placement of the apostrophe.

Exercise 5: Money

During the preview, you may want to read some of these sayings aloud and ask students to put them in their own words. Explain the ones they don't understand.

If students offer sound reasons for checking adages with which you might disagree, consider their answers correct. This suggestion also applies to their interpretations of the adages about which they choose to write. As a follow-up writing activity, students can select a saying that they believe is true and explain why they think so.

Exercise 6: More about Money

During the preview, read the poem aloud to the students. Be especially supportive in your critique of the students' answers during the homework review. Many students have a rather negative attitude toward poetry; any encouraging remarks you can make about their ability to interpret it will help them to approach poetry with a more positive attitude.

Lesson 14

A Ride in Space

Primary emphasis

- Reading comprehension (article)
- Understanding a cartoon
- Distinguishing between fact and opinion
- Using context clues

Secondary emphasis

- The prefix *re-*
- Compound words
- The singular possessive

Words for Study

Because many students are unfamiliar with space flight terminology, you may want to discuss many of the new words during the homework preview. A brief discussion about how new fields bring new words into our everyday language is helpful. The automobile revolution or computer technology provide good examples with which students are already familiar.

Reading Selection

To introduce the reading, tell students that Sally Ride was the first American woman astronaut. Point out that this selection is a condensation from a magazine article rather than an excerpt from a longer work.

Exercise 2: Understanding Cartoons

A good follow-up activity for this exercise is to have students bring in cartoons from the editorial page of their local newspaper to analyze. Because *fact* and *opinion* are discussed in this lesson, you may want to consider discussing the purpose of the editorial page and reading sections from it in class.

Exercise 3: Facts and Opinions

Most students have little difficulty with this exercise. What they do have trouble with, however, is recognizing that many of the statements they make are opinions, but that they say them as if they were facts. Of course, it is not just reading students who confuse fact with opinion in daily conversation. Adults especially find discussing this confusion between fact and opinion helpful.

Exercise 5: More Work with the Apostrophe

If students are still having difficulty forming the singular possessive, have them refer to Exercise 4 in the previous lesson.

Exercise 6: Compound Words

Even though students are familiar with this type of exercise, some of these compound words may be unfamiliar. Remind them to use the process of elimination

and to look up the words in List A in a dictionary. *Windbreakers*, in number 4, should be capitalized because it is a trademark.

Lesson 15

New York to France—in a Rowboat

Primary emphasis

- Reading comprehension (article)
- Distinguishing between fact and opinion
- Finding information in reference books

Secondary emphasis

- Using context clues
- The prefix *pre-*
- Classifying information
- Vocabulary (synonyms and antonyms)

Reading Selection

To introduce this reading, have a globe or a world map available and point out New York harbor and the coast of France, so that students can get an idea of the extent of this journey they will read about.

As a follow-up activity, students can write about a great adventure they would like to participate in. Encourage them to give free rein to their imaginations.

Exercise 1: About the Reading

Because students have not completed this type of exercise previously in this series, spend some time during the homework preview helping them to develop a pattern for their responses.

Exercise 2: What Do You Think?

For students who say they cannot respond to the question because they would not risk their lives for any kind of fortune, encourage them to explain their point of view in detail.

By now, most students have shown considerable improvement in their writing, and this exercise usually provides you with an excellent opportunity to point this out to them. If they accuse you of "buttering them up," refer them to their writing in the earlier lessons in the book.

Exercise 6: Bodies of Water

Make sure students note the suggestion in the directions during the homework preview. The suggestion pertains to questions 2 and 3. A dictionary with a good geographical section will probably contain all the information needed to complete this exercise, but students with smaller abridged dictionaries may need to consult an encyclopedia or atlas for some of the answers.

Review: Lessons 1-15

As with other reviews, students are not to consider this as a test, but as an opportunity to review words and concepts that have been introduced in the preceding lessons. An overall score of 80% or better on a review exercise should be considered excellent.

Exercise 6: Five-Letter Words

The only difficulty students might have in completing this review is getting started with this puzzle. You may want to help students complete a few of the items during the homework preview.

Tell students to skip around, to skim, and to use the sums as clues. For example, most students know that the answer for clue 3 is *devil*. Ask them what letter of this word is least used. Their response is usually *v*, which is correct. Tell them to skim the puzzle for a word with a *v*. Sure enough, they will spot *lived*, and they have the correct space. Remind them that the *d* is to be written on the third blank below the clues because it is the third clue. If they fill in the blanks for the largest inland sea as they go along, they may guess the answer before the puzzle is finished. This, in turn, will give them the initial letters of the remaining words.

Also point out to them that the clue numbers always add up to 34, both horizontally and vertically. This may help them to find the right answers and also to know whether or not they have the right answers.

Lesson 16

As American As Apple Pie
Primary emphasis
- Reading comprehension (nonfiction)
- Using context clues
- Words with multiple meanings

Secondary emphasis
- Reading Middle English
- The suffix -*tion*
- Forming the plural possessive

Reading Selection

During the preview, note the division marked by the asterisks and explain to the students that this reading consists of two distinct parts. An interesting follow-up discussion can center on which of the statements about Johnny Appleseed are probably true and which are probably the product of imagination.

Exercise 2: A Recipe for Apple Fritters

During the preview, have students note the strange spellings of the words in the recipe and explain that this is an example of English as spoken and written from the 12th to the 15th centuries. Assure them that with the help of context clues and the questions they will be able to figure out most of the words.

During the review, have students attempt to read the recipe aloud. If possible, bring in other samples of Middle English for them to see. "The Cuckoo Song," which begins "Sumer is icumen in/Lhude sing cuccu," is a good example, or any part of Chaucer's *Canterbury Tales* in the original version.

Exercise 3: Words with More Than One Meaning

Be sure students understand that all of the answer choices are correct meanings for the underlined word, but that only one is correct in the context of the sentence.

Exercise 6: The Unfruitful Reunion

Some of the "fruitful" expressions may be obscure to the students. For instance, they may not be familiar with the slang meanings for *rhubarb* and *raspberry*, or the expression to "give a fig." If they approach the exercise in a spirit of fun, they should be able to figure out most of the answers.

Have students read the dialogue aloud. As an additional writing activity, students may want to create their own dialogues. After any necessary revisions, they can then select a partner and read their dialogues to the class.

Lesson 17

Save Your Stomach
Primary emphasis
- Reading comprehension (nonfiction)
- Main ideas and supporting details
- Forming a reasoned opinion
- Using a calorie chart

Secondary emphasis
- Using context clues
- Vocabulary (word review)
- The suffix -*sion*
- Forming the plural possessive

Words for Study

Note that *St.* is the abbreviation for both *Saint* and *Street*.

Reading Selection

To introduce this reading, a simple drawing of the human alimentary canal is helpful. Such a drawing can be found in most encyclopedias. Find out if students can locate their own stomachs. During the discussion, ask students if they learned facts they hadn't known before about their stomachs and their eating habits.

A suggested follow-up activity is to have the students keep track of their own "food contacts" for a day or a week and write a report or have a class discussion on their findings.

Exercise 1: According to the Author

Since this is an unfamiliar exercise format, allow as much time during the preview as necessary to be sure students understand how to do it. Remind them to check the reading when they are unsure of where the supporting details belong.

Exercise 5: Counting Calories

During the preview, make sure students can read the chart. Give them a chance to skim through it and react to anything that may surprise them. During the review, have a class discussion about question 10.

Lesson 18

A Breakfast Scene
Primary emphasis

- Comprehension of literature (drama)
- Colloquialisms
- Forming a reasoned opinion

Secondary emphasis

- Using context clues
- Vocabulary (synonyms and antonyms)
- Forming singular and plural possessives
- The suffixes -ance and -ence

Words for Study

Because this scene from *A Raisin in the Sun* could not be adapted but had to be excerpted in its entirety, the vocabulary for this lesson is a bit more difficult than usual. Preview the new words carefully and discuss the meanings of those which are new to the students. Not all the new words have been listed. Other new words include *conspicuously, sullen, vindicated, rigidity,* and *finality.* Even if students are not familiar with the definitions for these words, they should not have too much difficulty with the pronunciations. Your assessment of students' ability to handle all this new vocabulary should determine whether to discuss these words during the preview or to help your students discern their meanings as questions arise.

The Scene

In introducing the scene, it may be wise to point out that in addition to new vocabulary, the dialogue is in the vernacular, and some of the phrasing may be unfamiliar to some students. Point out the stage directions in parentheses and italics and explain that while these words are not spoken aloud, they should be read, since they give

clues to the action of the scene and to the characters' feelings. Explain that this scene takes place near the beginning of the play.

During the homework review, students enjoy reading the dialogue aloud and sharing their answers to the comprehension questions.

As a follow-up activity, you might read Langston Hughes's poem "Harlem" and discuss its relationship to the play (the play's title comes from this poem).

Exercise 3: Food for Thought

During the review, ask the students how many of these expressions they already knew, how many they were able to figure out by using "common sense" and how many required "intelligent guessing" and the process of elimination. This type of mini-survey reminds them that there is usually more than one road to the right answer.

Exercise 5: The Suffixes -ance and -ence

As a reinforcement activity, plan a brief spelling quiz on -ance and -ence words to help students improve their ability to distinguish between these two spellings.

Lesson 19

Taste Treats
Primary emphasis

- Reading comprehension (nonfiction)
- Forming a reasoned opinion
- Classifying information

Secondary emphasis

- Word families
- A review of singular and plural possessives
- Reasoning and spelling (Can You Crack the Code?)

Words for Study

Note the abbreviation *Inc.* and be sure students know what it stands for.

Reading Selection

In introducing the reading, draw attention to the subheadings and briefly note their purpose. You may want to draw students' attention to the title of the work this excerpt was taken from. "You Are What You Eat" should sound familiar to students. The German phrase "Man is what he eats" was mentioned in the reading for Lesson 17.

During the review, discuss whether or not students think the food they eat is good for them. Follow-up writing activity topics include: "Why I Eat What I Eat," "How My Eating Habits Have Changed," "My Favorite Food," "My Favorite Meal," etc.

Exercise 1: About the Reading

Briefly discuss question 8. Draw students' attention to the fact that the title of the reading selection and the sentence from the selection are also in quotation marks, and ask them to give the reasons for these marks, also.

Exercise 2: What Do You Think?

Have students read their responses aloud and discuss them.

Exercise 3: A Taste Test

There may be some disagreement about how to classify some of the items. Mention that we are not born with these taste categories; they are learned, and therefore opinions may differ. Some people confuse sour and bitter, for instance.

Exercise 6: Can You Crack the Code?

Remind students that they did a similar puzzle in Lesson 7. Students enjoy seeing pictures of these jewels, if you can find them.

Lesson 20
The Wizard of Alabama
Primary emphasis

- Reading comprehension (biography)
- Forming a reasoned opinion
- Using context clues
- Comprehension of literature (poem)

Secondary emphasis

- Analogies (word relationships)
- The suffix -ize
- Vocabulary review (puzzle)

Reading Selection

To introduce this reading, you may want to review the term *biography*. Ask if students have heard of George Washington Carver, and if they know why he is remembered.

During the review, consider having this selection read aloud. Take some time to discuss Carver's life and contributions. You may want to have students create a list of adjectives such as *modest, unselfish, wise*, etc., that describe Carver.

Exercise 2: More Facts about the Peanut

This is not an easy exercise. Remind students to read the entire sentence before trying to select the word that fits best and to use context clues. Also, remind them to read the entire passage after filling in the blanks. Be sure students capitalize the word *Pegs*.

Exercise 5: Find This Peanut Product

Remind students that they did a similar puzzle in the Review of Lessons 1-5 and refer them to that if necessary.

Exercise 6: To Look at Any Thing

During the preview, read the poem aloud to the students. The answers to questions 1 and 4 must be inferred from the poem and the reading. It is a good idea to review the process of making inferences during the preview.

Allow ample time to discuss the students' responses to these questions during the review. Emphasize the strengths and note the weaknesses in students' writing progress.

Review: Lessons 1-20

As with the other review lessons, remind students that this is not a test but a final opportunity to review words and concepts that were introduced in this book.

Emphasize improvement in the students' work habits, reasoning, and vocabulary development during the homework review.

Students generally experience a sense of accomplishment (and relief) upon completing a workbook, and they should have a few moments to enjoy and evaluate this accomplishment before continuing their studies.

If you wish to use one last follow-up activity, here are two suggestions:

1. Have students write an opinion, supported with details, about how they believe completing this book has or has not helped them in their reading and writing development.

2. Have them write their own version of Exercise 6 for fellow students to complete.

Answer Key for Book 6

Lesson 1

1 About the Reading

1. In real life, the wounds were much more serious, and good medical help was scarce.
2. In real life, a large number of bullet wounds were in the abdomen or chest.
3. In real life, a shoulder wound can be extremely harmful or even fatal.
4. In reality, gunfighters were often shot in the face.
5. In real life, the victim often staggered backward twelve feet before falling to the ground.
6. Many times men were shot in the back or without ever having a chance to shoot back.

What do you think? Answers will vary. Accept any reasonable response.

2 Which Word Does Not Fit?

1. liver	5. diameter	9. exhausted
2. crisp	6. affect	10. convinced
3. suffer	7. excited	11. plead
4. haul	8. occur	12. petty

3 Words That End with -ment

1. shipment	5. commitment	9. advancement
2. enlargement	6. ailment	10. encouragement
3. engagement	7. management	11. discouragement
4. measurement	8. enjoyment	12. confinement

4 Who Was Wild Bill Hickok?

served, officer, thieves, defending, duty, certainly, included
afternoon, Several, refused, continued, strolled
murderer, badly, insisted, breakfast

5 Spelling

1. thieves	5. leaves	9. wives
2. calves	6. loaves	10. knives
3. elves	7. shelves	
4. halves	8. selves	

Lesson 2

1 About the Reading

1. Oklahoma
2. ancestors
3. thought he was a strange-looking baby
4. physicians
5. he forgot about them while he was in office
6. oil was discovered on their land
7. restless
8. it gave him an opportunity to learn new things
9. gunfighter
10. eight

2 Arithmetic Problem

56 years old

3 What Do You Think?

Answers will vary.

4 Pleasure

1. mysteries	5. worrying	9. touchdowns
2. tips	6. wisecracks	10. beaches
3. libraries	7. knowledge	11. blood
4. gossip	8. strikeouts	12. broomsticks

5 Displeasure

1. alarms	5. train wrecks	9. hisses and boos
2. bears	6. weeds	10. haste
3. confinement	7. grease and grime	11. budgets
4. potholes	8. cave-ins	12. daybreak

6 More Work with the Ending -ment

1. punishment	5. retirement	9. Detachment
2. employment	6. wonderment	10. misplacement
3. requirement	7. mistreatment	11. concealment
4. involvement	8. government	12. settlement

7 The Capitol and Capitals

1. Denver	5. Lansing	9. Oklahoma City
2. Honolulu	6. Jackson	10. Columbia
3. Springfield	7. Trenton	11. Nashville
4. Boston	8. Columbus	12. Salt Lake City

Lesson 3

1 About the Reading

1. d	4. a	7. b	10. a
2. b	5. a	8. d	11. d
3. d	6. a	9. c	12. c

2 Synonyms

1. vessel	5. requirement	9. ailment
2. ceaseless	6. uneasily	10. nowadays
3. raring	7. enjoyment	11. popular
4. occurrence	8. commitment	12. employment

3 Antonyms

1. disappear
2. conceal
3. confinement
4. persist
5. detachment
6. short-lived
7. unpopular
8. irregular
9. movement
10. separately
11. standard
12. serious

4 Spelling

1. sleepiness
2. ugliness
3. dizziness
4. liveliness
5. nastiness
6. loveliness
7. dustiness
8. greasiness
9. holiness
10. uneasiness

5 Words That End with -ness

1. fondness
2. loudness
3. rudeness
4. forgiveness
5. gracefulness
6. awareness
7. eagerness
8. stillness
9. greatness
10. forgetfulness
11. calmness
12. seriousness

6 Capitalization Rules: Part 1

1. John, Mary, Cape, Cod, Thousand, Islands
2. On, Fourth, July, Ohio, River
3. Roger, South, America, Africa, Europe
4. Mrs., Price, Christmas, October, Thanksgiving
5. On, Good, Friday, Dr., Lodge, Chestnut, Street
6. When, Kate, Carver, City, Hospital, Riverside, Lane
7. Ruth, Andrew, Jackson, England, Monday
8. Buddy, August, Great, Smoky, Mountains, Dr., Carpenter
9. Mr., Knight, Rosebud, Lane, Columbia, South, Carolina
10. I, I, Honolulu, I, Vermont, Uncle, Steven

Lesson 4

1 About the Story

1. Martha is in a good mood; she is happy and expectant.
2. Paul is also in a good mood, since he agrees to go to the World Playhouse rather than their usual movie theater, the Owl.
3. Paul acts nervous and uncomfortable. He feels out of place because they are the only blacks there.
4. Martha hates to have Paul act and feel inferior to white people.
5. Martha seems to enjoy being in the kind of theater white people go to. It makes her feel rich, as if she were part of a different way of life.
6. Paul feels more comfortable, as though he belongs there. This is probably because they were allowed to go in and are now a part of the audience, and also because it is dark.
7. Answers will vary. Accept any reasonable response.
8. Answers will vary. Accept any reasonable response.
9. The story was written years ago. Martha seemed to consider Technicolor special. They referred to themselves as "colored people." They would probably not be the only black people in most movie theaters today. The story's copyright date is 1953.

2 Synonyms

1. separate
2. engagement
3. loveliness
4. continuously
5. usually
6. protest
7. precise
8. instance
9. cinema
10. mercy
11. eagerness
12. recently

3 Antonyms

1. dull
2. clumsiness
3. softness
4. sinfulness
5. discouraged
6. imagined
7. politeness
8. bold
9. commotion
10. beauty
11. rarely
12. coolly

4 More Work with the Ending -ness

1. freshness
2. politeness
3. smoothness
4. stiffness
5. dullness
6. dryness
7. plumpness
8. truthfulness
9. bitterness
10. gentleness

5 Spelling

1. thirstiness
2. riskiness
3. craziness
4. dirtiness
5. noisiness
6. nosiness
7. bloodiness
8. clumsiness
9. scratchiness
10. itchiness
11. faultiness
12. sneakiness

6 Capitalization Rules: Part 2

1. When, Holiday, Inn, Mr., Holland, Greek, Forest, Avenue
2. Adam, Super, Bowl, Dallas, Cowboys
3. Ms., Woods, Huron, Indians, Spring, Valley, Public, Library, Pueblo, Indians
4. When, Ford, Bush, County, Courthouse, Louis, Standard, Savings, Loan
5. The, Free, Ride, Insurance, Company, Dr., Springfield, Rolls, Royce, Roger's, Fish, Market, Perch, Street
6. I, Mr., Brooks, Steven, Jell-O, Tuesday, War
7. When, Jackson, Washington, D.C., Capitol, Congress
8. While, Tony, Aunt, Martha, Springfield, Falls, Road, Middle, School

Lesson 5

1 About the Reading

1. Jackie's grandmother controlled Jackie, and he was wary of her because she slapped him when he didn't obey directions. He didn't mind the slapping as much as he had minded it when she had pinched him, however.
2. His uncle, the director, tricked him by making him think that his part was being given to another boy who was dressed in the Skippy costume.
3. The director pretended to order the security guard to shoot Jackie's dog. The guard went out to where Jackie's grandmother had taken the dog, and then a shot was heard.

What do you think? Answers will vary. This is what actually happened. Jackie's mother went with him the day the third crying scene was to be filmed. She explained the scene to Jackie, telling him what had happened to Skippy and why he was crying. As they talked, Jackie reports, "I began to cry because now I knew and I sympathized and I cried honest tears. Still crying, I went out and took my place, and it was all done in one take."

2 Compound Words

1. standby	5. birthstone	9. roundabout
2. outnumbered	6. turtleneck	10. freehand
3. outspoken	7. thunderclouds	11. bookkeeper
4. stomachache	8. timetable	12. clockwork

3 Word Families

1. imagination, imagine
2. concentration, concentrate
3. operator, operated, operation
4. assistant, assistance, assist
5. security, insecure, secure
6. adventurous, adventurously, adventure
7. Desperate, desperation, desperately
8. persisted, persistent, persistence
9. resentment, resentfully, resentful, resents
10. appearance, disappearance, disappeared, appear

4 Tears

eyelids, ducts, emotion, anger, fluid, occur

layer, dust, cornea, result

5 Capitalization Review

1. the merry month of May
2. a roll of cherry Life Savers
3. 620 Riverside Drive
4. her French book
5. the U.S. Justice Department
6. a bowl of Cheerios
7. the University of Iowa
8. the Roaring Twenties
9. a Dodge truck
10. Halloween pranks
11. the Canadian flag
12. the Oklahoma State Fair

Review: Lessons 1-5

1 Word Review

1. tendon	9. Capitol
2. tantrum	10. Salt Lake City
3. statue	11. Thomas A. Edison
4. wallop	12. Alaska
5. yelp	13. dialogue
6. cornea	14. Mississippi
7. habit	15. Andrew Jackson
8. Cherokee	

2 Synonyms and Antonyms

1. synonyms	6. synonyms	11. antonyms
2. antonyms	7. antonyms	12. synonyms
3. synonyms	8. synonyms	13. synonyms
4. antonyms	9. antonyms	14. antonyms
5. synonyms	10. antonyms	15. antonyms

3 Suffixes

1. instructor	5. urgently	9. instructions
2. inventor	6. seriously	10. concentration
3. saltiness	7. persistence	
4. usefulness	8. appearance	

4 Where Might You Find These?

1. theaters	9. Mississippi
2. mines	10. Michigan
3. Oklahoma	11. horror movies
4. concert halls	12. cameras
5. Capitol building	13. holsters
6. state capitals	14. track meets
7. graveyards	15. kennels
8. Europe	

5 Review of Capitalization Rules

Answers will vary.

6 Compound Words

1. checkerboard	5. manpower	9. oddball
2. officeholder	6. blackjack	10. hitchhiker
3. leftover	7. upbringing	11. inkblot
4. underclothes	8. sandman	12. offspring

City: Columbus
State: Ohio

Lesson 6

1 About the Reading

1. b	3. c	5. d	7. a
2. b	4. a	6. c	8. d

2 What Do You Think?

Answers will vary.

3 Synonyms

1. own	5. lately	9. dejected
2. uncertain	6. frighten	10. disperse
3. disgraced	7. relaxed	11. lesson
4. allow	8. change	12. idea

4 The Suffix -ful

1. scoopful	4. forceful
2. playful	5. regretful, plateful
3. eventful, fearful	

5 The Suffix -less

1. shameless
2. heartless
3. ageless
4. meaningless, blameless
5. fearless, mindless

6 Review of Capitalization Rules

1. October, Black, Tuesday, American, Wall, Street, New, York, City
2. During, Depression, Washington, United, States
3. In, Chicago, Illinois
4. In, Uncle, Robert, Campbell's, Ritz
5. Not, Great, Depression, In, Georgia, Negro, In, New, York, Indian
6. A, Texas, As, I, I've
7. On, December, Americans, Japanese, Pearl, Harbor, Hawaii, Shortly, Congress, Japan
8. The, Great, Depression, Congress, United, States, World, War

Lesson 7

1 About the Reading

1. d	3. a	5. d	7. d
2. a	4. c	6. b	8. b

An arithmetic problem: 1824

2 Symbols

First set:
1. striped pole
2. CO_2
3. yellow
4. four-leaf clover
5. scales
6. ♫
7. O
8. skull and crossbones
9. broken mirror
10. Uncle Sam

Second set:
1. bat
2. bee or ant
3. beaver
4. lamb
5. dove
6. eel
7. fox
8. ox or bull
9. mule
10. owl

3 Word Families

1. election, elected
2. adjustments, adjust
3. reference, refer
4. prefer, preference
5. slippery, slipperiness
6. hearty, heartily, heartless
7. stubborn, stubbornly, stubbornness
8. application, applicant, applied
9. cowardliness, cowardly, coward
10. usual, usually, unusually, unusual

4 Looking for a Job

1. a. Monday   d. appointment
   b. Friday   e. between
   c. September   f. and
2. Busboys at Rolling Hills Country Club
3. Construction "Jack-of-all-Trades" and Manager for ladies' sportswear shop
4. Personal appearance and/or personality are probably important for the job, and the interviewer wants an opportunity to judge these factors.
5. Answers will vary.

5 Can You Crack the Code?

1. James Polk
2. George Washington
3. John F. Kennedy
4. John Quincy Adams
5. Andrew Jackson
6. Abraham Lincoln
7. John Adams
8. Thomas Jefferson
9. James Madison
10. James Monroe

Lesson 8

1 About the Reading

2. When looking for a job, you should seek the support of other job-hunters and your friends.
3. You should know what you want to do and state it exactly so that the decision about what you can or cannot do is not made by others.
4. You should contact companies you would like to work for whether or not they have advertised job openings, because they are often looking for potential new employees.
5. (blank)
6. Decide where you want to work and concentrate your job search on that area, because there are jobs around.
7. (blank)
8. Research a company thoroughly before going for an interview or filling out an application, and then approach the person who has the power to hire you.

2 Jobs

1. screenwriter
2. stockbroker
3. middleman
4. stationmaster
5. locksmith
6. typesetter
7. beekeeper
8. brakeman
9. floorwalker
10. lumberjack
11. nursemaid
12. cowpuncher

3 Antonyms

1. victory
2. guilty
3. level
4. important
5. impolite
6. unnecessary
7. imagined
8. shameless
9. vague
10. old
11. gentle
12. wastefulness

4 The Suffix -ly

1. d	3. a	5. a	7. d	9. a
2. c	4. b	6. b	8. c	10. b

5 More Work with the Suffix -ly

1. angrily	5. mightily	9. dreamily
2. heartily	6. worthily	10. unworthily
3. merrily	7. steadily	11. guiltily
4. cheerily	8. crazily	12. moodily

6 Capitalization Rules: Part 3

1. In, English, Thursday, Mr., Fisher, *A, Tale, Two, Cities*, Monday
2. While, South, Trentons, Stony, Brook, Motel, Beech, Avenue, Memphis
3. Francis, Scott, Key, The, Star-Spangled, Banner, War, British
4. When, Peggy, Hickock, County, *Grand, Island, Daily, Times*
5. Mrs., Ritz, Department, Transportation, Washington, D.C., New, England
6. Upon, Smothers, Business, College, Louise, Mick, Just, Typing, Typing, Walnut, Hills, High, School
7. Mr., East, North, Street, South, Street, West, Branch, Savings, Loan
8. When, Jesse, Christianity, Judaism, Islam, Bible, Talmud, Koran
9. The, American, Red, Cross, Sons, Italy, Moosewood, City, Hall
10. Leafing, *Family, Circle*, June, Jefferson, Boston, Helping, Hand, Club's

7 A Skills Survey

Answers will vary. Accept all reasonable responses.

Lesson 9

1 About the Reading

1. c	3. a	5. c	7. c
2. d	4. d	6. d	8. a

2 Positive and Negative

Answers will vary. Reasonable responses include:

2. *Positive*: Select your outfit carefully, making sure your clothes are clean, neat and business-like, and that they look good on you.
   Negative: Think, "It really doesn't matter what I wear because I probably won't get the job anyway."
3. *Positive*: Describe clearly the things you do well, any training you have had, and any experience you have that may apply to this particular job.
   Negative: Act unsure of what you can do or say, "I really don't have any experience, but I can probably learn to do most anything."
4. *Positive*: Mention a salary figure near the top of the salary range for this job (which you have researched in advance).
   Negative: Say you don't really know what salary you want.

5. *Positive*: Remember that the interview itself was a good learning experience which will help you to do better the next time.
   Negative: Give up trying to find a job because you know you'll never get one.

3 How Would You Classify This?

1. state	5. transportation	9. measurement
2. machinery	6. supervisor	10. timepiece
3. income	7. promise	11. emotion
4. social event	8. crime	12. symbol

4 More Work with Classifications

Days	Languages	Measurements
Fri.	Eng.	gal.
Mon.	Fr.	lb.
Sat.	Ital.	oz.
Thurs.	Jap.	pt.
Wed.	Rus.	qt.

States	Months
AL	Aug.
CA	Dec.
MA	Jan.
NY	Mar.
WA	Sept.

5 More Work with the Suffix -ly

1. legally	6. useless	11. social
2. positive	7. popularly	12. negatively
3. immediate	8. separate	13. individually
4. fearlessly	9. impolite	14. previously
5. currently	10. useful	15. realistically

6 Filling out an Employment Application

Answers will vary.

Lesson 10

1 About the Story

1. Life seemed "hollow and a burden" because Tom had to paint a fence on a beautiful summer Saturday.
2. He had managed to get other people to pay him to let them paint the fence.
3. Once his tactic had worked on that boy the rest was easy.
4. Tom was playing "hard to get" and making it seem as though he took pride in the job and enjoyed doing it.
5. The "law of human action" Tom used was that to make someone want something badly, you make it difficult to get.
6. Work is something you have to do, and play is something you don't have to do.
7. Answers will vary.
8. Answers will vary.

2 If Only Someone Else Would Do It!

1. dressmaker	5. stationmaster	9. cowpuncher
2. student	6. butcher	10. scribe
3. teacher	7. lifeguard	
4. floorwalker	8. treasurer	

Answers will vary on the last two questions.

3 Word Relationships

1. b	3. a	5. d	7. b	9. d
2. b	4. c	6. d	8. c	10. a

4 Review of Suffixes

1. judgment	6. purely	11. bareness
2. contentment	7. scornful	12. innocently
3. merciless	8. vagueness	13. limitless
4. blankness	9. merciful	14. childless
5. vastly	10. dutiful	15. misjudgment

5 Spelling

1. differences	5. your	9. can't
2. lightning	6. starving	10. promise
3. possession	7. hundred	11. thankful
4. somebody	8. cabbages	12. experience

6 What Exactly Is a Jew's-Harp?

incorrectly, consists, create, finger

traveled, concerts, damaged, dentist, resume, instrument

Europe, glory, popular, Asia, gentlemen

Review: Lessons 1-10

1 Word Review

1. interview	5. crisis	9. felony
2. suffix	6. experiment	10. applicant
3. prefix	7. Mark Twain	11. roll call
4. whitewash	8. United Nations	12. Abraham Lincoln

2 Word Review

1. symbol	5. unstructured	9. heartiness
2. impression	6. dependable	10. indicated
3. minor	7. fierce	11. inspiration
4. scorned	8. resumed	12. particular

3 Compound Words

1. corncob, haystack	5. signpost, sideswiped
2. scatterbrain, airline	6. aftertaste, mouthwash
3. fiddlesticks, cookout	7. waterfront, seasick
4. staircase, checkmate	8. lifelong, masterpiece

4 Review of Capitalization Rules

Answers will vary.

5 Looking for a Job

1.
a. references	e. preferred
b. transportation	f. available
c. weekly	g. company
d. responsible	h. license

2. 555-3141 and 555-2747
3. It means the position pays an hourly wage, and in addition there is a commission paid on sales made.
4. Any of the following: Baby Sitter Needed; Barmaid, Waitress & Porter; Child Care; Cleaners; Driver; Pet Shop Clerk; Photo Store; Sales Help for Craft Store; Sales—Weekends Pet Shop; Service Agent; Telephone Sales; Telephone Sales & Appointments; Typist; Waiters—Waitresses
5. Any of the following: Control Desk Person; Presser; Sales—Weekend Pet Shop; Service Agent Position
6. Equal Opportunity Employer

What do you think? Answers will vary.

6 Find the Quote

1. penknife		7. lighthouse
2. New Year's Eve		8. tadpole
3. positive		9. daddy
4. teakettle		10. artery
5. Honolulu		11. engineer
6. thirteen		12. wallflower

Quote: The only thing people in every walk of life will agree on is that they are underpaid and overworked.

Lesson 11

1 About the Reading

1. **Cause and Effect**
    1. the barber was stunned.
    2. the captain was unhurt.
    3. he returned to help rescue the wounded.
    4. he begged the others to shoot him.
    5. the wounded were taken to Memphis.
    6. the physicians gave him less attention.
    7. Memphis knew how to respond to the accident.
    8. patients for whom there was no hope were taken to the death room.
    9. the chief mate refused both medicine and water.
    10. he was able to work again as a mate on a steamboat.
2. **What do you think?** Answers will vary. Accept any reasonable response.

2 Synonyms and Antonyms

1. moored, adrift		7. unending, passing
2. naked, clothed		8. precisely, vaguely
3. abuse, tenderness		9. seep, gush
4. offspring, ancestors		10. faultless, incorrect
5. ruin, create		11. formerly, currently
6. compliment, insult		12. active, idle

3 Idle Threats

1. intend, contend, extend, attend
2. preview, review, overview, interview
3. devise, revise, advise, supervise
4. admit, commit, transmit, submit
5. reserve, conserve, deserve, preserve
6. impose, dispose, compose, expose
7. depress, compress, express, impress
8. extract, contract, detract, subtract

4 Contractions

1. isn't
2. I'm
3. don't
4. doesn't
5. didn't
6. she's
7. it's
8. I'd
9. I'll
10. he'll
11. you're
12. you've

5 Traveling by Steamboat

1. cabins
2. People usually dress up for dinner.
3. The boat would stop at the nearest shore stop to get a doctor.
4. your own insurance or travel agent
5. Bathroom doorways are not wide enough for wheelchairs.
6. nothing (They are provided by the steamboat company.)
7. on the sun deck
8. any of the following: wine, photographs, gifts
9. The ticket describes the legal contract between the company and the passenger.
10. Answers will vary.

Lesson 12

1 About the Reading

1. d
2. d
3. a
4. b
5. c
6. a
7. a
8. c
9. c
10. d

2 What Do You Think?

Answers will vary.

3 Word Relationships

1. disaster is to tragic
2. taut is to slack
3. drill is to dentist's office
4. alter is to revise
5. train is to engine
6. North Carolina is to the South
7. sober is to silly
8. mph is to abbreviation
9. bloom is to wilt
10. parachute is to airplane

4 The Prefix *un-*

1. untrue
2. undesirable
3. uninterested
4. uninformed
5. unfastened
6. unfruitful
7. unexpected
8. unleashed
9. unskilled
10. Unsafe
11. ungrateful
12. unlimited

5 More Work with Contractions

1. we'd
2. they'd
3. she'll
4. he'll
5. we're
6. they've
7. he's
8. how's
9. there's
10. hasn't
11. weren't
12. ma'am

Lesson 13

1 About the Story

1. d
2. a
3. c
4. b
5. c
6. d
7. a
8. b
9. c
10. a

2 More Prefixes That Mean *Not*

1. impure
2. indigestion
3. illegal
4. irresponsible
5. inexperience
6. nonmetal
7. independent
8. indirect
9. nonskid
10. Improper
11. Indecent
12. insane
13. Nonsense
14. impatient

3 A Fat Boy without Any Clothes On

arrows, pierced
wildness, supposed, create, reject
deadly, perched
bowstring, eyes
sprinted, escape, prayed, plea
sorry, crown

4 The Apostrophe to Show Ownership

1. Polly's impression
2. the cheerleader's uniform
3. the actress's costume
4. the morphine's effects
5. Mrs. Mack's coffeecake
6. the screenwriter's masterpiece
7. the angel's wings
8. the beekeeper's hives
9. the chief's discovery
10. Jackie's tantrums
11. the earth's atmosphere
12. the psychiatrist's patients

5 Money

Answers to both parts of this question will vary. Accept any reasonable responses.

6 **More about Money**

1. doesn't do anything serious; is silly; wastes time
2. one's fate; one's place in life
3. The poet seems to agree with Anthony Rockwall, because he says that he'd change places with a rich man.
4. Answers will vary.

Lesson 14

1 **About the Reading**

1. b	3. d	5. a	7. a	9. d
2. d	4. c	6. b	8. c	

2 **Understanding Cartoons**

1. Sally's role as a woman
2. the noses; because the reporters are being nosy
3. She is angry. This is indicated by the black cloud over her head as she turns her back on them and walks away.
4. The cartoonist seems to be on Sally's side because the reporters' questions are stupid and sexist.
5. Yes, because the reading passage quoted similar questions that Sally was asked by the press.
6. Yes. The reading indicated that reporters hounded her about being a woman and complained about not being able to get much information from her. The cartoonist shows her walking away from the reporters and refusing to answer their stupid questions.

3 **Facts and Opinions**

1. opinion	5. opinion	9. opinion
2. fact	6. fact	10. opinion
3. fact	7. opinion	
4. opinion	8. fact	

4 **The Prefix re-**

1. reopen	5. rephrased	9. reclaim
2. retracing	6. repossess	10. revoking
3. reunion	7. reconstruct	
4. recount	8. redouble	

5 **More Work with the Apostrophe**

1. the butcher's apron
2. Manhattan's skyline
3. Tony's cousins
4. the Volkswagen's radiator
5. Jack's fractured arm
6. the gerbil's cage
7. Francis's journey
8. Mr. Royal's servants
9. the satellite's orbit
10. the clinic's lounge
11. the veterinarian's routine
12. the angel's halo

6 **Compound Words**

1. daredevil, ripcord
2. rosebush, tombstone
3. tightwad, lookout
4. Windbreakers, motorboat
5. heavyweight, roadwork
6. wardrobe, homecoming
7. handyman, candlelight
8. overjoyed, guesswork

Lesson 15

1 **About the Reading**

1. Opinion: They meant that they would make it to France or die in the attempt, but they didn't actually expect to see all the people in France or in heaven.
2. Fact: Harbo had felt the bump of a shark against the bottom of the boat.
3. Opinion: Harbo couldn't know ahead of time whether or not they could clear the giant wave, even though it turned out that he was right.
4. Opinion: The men were not intending to commit suicide.
5. Opinion: They thought they would earn a lot of money rowing across the ocean, but they were wrong.
6. Opinion: The reporter felt that Samuelson had been an unusually brave and adventurous man.

2 **What Do You Think?**

Answers will vary.

3 **Synonyms**

1. bulletin	5. furthermore	9. glorious
2. illegal	6. agreement	10. conflict
3. suspect	7. decrease	11. consideration
4. occupation	8. faraway	12. nerveless

4 **Antonyms**

1. ashore	5. disperse	9. remote
2. reckless	6. watertight	10. defense
3. irresponsible	7. abbreviate	11. inexperienced
4. retrieve	8. manmade	12. heavenly

5 **The Prefix pre-**

1. prejudged	5. preview	9. premedical
2. preheat	6. prewar	10. Prehistory
3. preschool	7. pretest	11. precooked
4. predated	8. preshrunk	12. prepay

6 Bodies of Water

1. A. sea B. lake C. river D. ocean
2.

Lakes	Oceans
Great Salt	Arctic
Huron	Atlantic
Louise	Indian
Michigan	Pacific

Rivers	Seas
Amazon	Caribbean
Mississippi	Dead
Nile	North
Snake	South China

3. a. the Nile
   b. the Pacific Ocean
   c. the Caribbean
   d. the Great Salt Lake
   e. Lake Louise

Review: Lessons 1-15

1 Word Review

1. capsule
2. morphine
3. compass
4. megaphone
5. Nile
6. Amazon
7. satellite
8. myth
9. shuttle
10. sextant
11. oilskin
12. reins
13. generation
14. Broadway
15. poverty

2 Word Review

1. d
2. b
3. d
4. c
5. c
6. b
7. b
8. a
9. a
10. d
11. d
12. a
13. d
14. d
15. b

3 How Would You Classify It?

1. astronaut
2. scarlet
3. barrel
4. rifle
5. kerosene
6. Cupid
7. sextant
8. whale
9. encyclopedia
10. cosmonaut
11. moon
12. Challenger
13. cinnamon
14. motorcycle

4 Facts and Opinions

Answers will vary.

5 Review of the Apostrophe and Capitalization

1. Ever since she'd read the story of Cupid in her brother's Greek mythology book, Kate wished that such a god really did exist who would shoot an arrow of passion into Dr. Springtime's heart.
2. "I'd meet you at Grand Central Station, but Manhattan's traffic is so bad you'd be better off just taking a taxi to West End Avenue," Adam told Aunt Mary, who was coming to visit for the weekend.
3. "They'll never have time to visit Grant's Tomb if they're planning to spend the afternoon in Central Park," said Tom who quickly added, "but then, who wants to see a tomb on such a glorious autumn afternoon."
4. After reading the article about Sally Ride's life in an old issue of *Time* magazine at the dentist's office, Tony was certain that her work on the Challenger had been much more relaxing than all the interviews she'd had to suffer through.

6 Five-Letter Words

MOORS 8 ROOMS	TUNAS 9 AUNTS	AMONG 1 MANGO	DREAD 16 ADDER
BELOW 2 ELBOW	FLIER 7 RIFLE	LEASE 15 EASEL	KNEAD 10 NAKED
HEART 11 EARTH	KNITS 14 STINK	RELAY 6 EARLY	LIVED 3 DEVIL
THORN 13 NORTH	ASIDE 4 IDEAS	RANGE 12 ANGER	BLEAT 5 TABLE

The world's largest inland sea: Mediterranean Sea

Lesson 16

1 About the Reading

1. b
2. b
3. c
4. a
5. d
6. a
7. c
8. b
9. a
10. d

2 A Recipe for Apple Fritters

1. Any five of the following: For, to, and, a, cast, fry, in, serve, it
2. A. take
   B. eggs
   C. batter
   D. pare
   E. cut
   F. them
   G. broad
   H. grease
3. A. fritters
   B. flour
   C. pepper
   D. make
   E. pieces
   F. fresh
4. Accept any reasonable guess, such as: There probably were no standard measurements at that time, or measuring cups and spoons were not available, etc.
5. Answers will vary.

3 Words with More Than One Meaning

1. a great number
2. a section of a hospital for the care of a particular group of patients
3. a group of assistants or workers
4. to question a sample group of people in order to survey public opinion
5. ghosts

6. to touch lightly in passing; to skim or brush
7. to annoy or upset
8. to put into action
9. a piece of such a material on which a painting is made, especially an oil painting
10. to give way to what is stronger or better

4 The Suffix -tion

1. accommodations
2. reservation
3. starvation
4. investigations
5. inflation
6. extractions
7. definitions
8. addiction
9. compositions
10. infections
11. exhaustion
12. explanations
13. temptation
14. graduation
15. combination

5 Using the Apostrophe with Plural Words

1. the colonies' growth
2. the players' defense
3. the rascals' pranks
4. the skyscrapers' construction
5. the bananas' ripeness
6. the cartoonists' dismissal
7. the Canadians' friendliness
8. the rockets' red glare
9. the visitors' entertainment
10. the daredevils' boldness
11. the motors' roar
12. the nurses' availability

6 The Unfruitful Reunion

date, grape, lemon, fig, strawberry, peach, Cherry, apple, banana, prune, rhubarb, lime, fruitcake, plum, Mulberry, raspberry

Lesson 17

1 According to the Author

2. a. One-sixth of all major illnesses are related to stomach disorders.
   b. One-half the population complains about their digestive systems.
   c. More than $350 million is spent each year on stomach medicine.
3. a. Many people eat no breakfast at all.
   b. Raiding the refrigerator in the middle of the night is common.
   c. Americans average about twenty "food contacts" a day.
4. a. Meals high in starch tend to empty out of the stomach more quickly.
   b. Meals high in fat tend to empty out of the stomach more slowly.

5. a. Constipation can be the result of depression.
   b. Diarrhea can be the result of anger.

2 Word Review

1. Pacific
2. wanderer
3. beaver
4. IOU
5. ulcer
6. mumps
7. cherries
8. hiss
9. easel
10. foxhole
11. moon
12. oil
13. 1800s
14. Midas
15. ragged

3 The Suffix -sion

1. division, profession
2. transfusion, permission
3. commission, conclusion
4. confusion, possession
5. impression, extension
6. revision, concussion
7. admission, invasion
8. omission, intermission
9. supervision, confession
10. transmission, decision

4 Using the Apostrophe with Plural Words

1. the chefs' recipes
2. the steel mills' output
3. the litterbugs' thoughtlessness
4. the strikers' settlement
5. the cowpunchers' saddles
6. the villagers' distrust
7. the roommates' possessions
8. the mountains' beauty
9. the researchers' findings
10. the sweethearts' affection

5 Counting Calories

1. ounce
2. inch
3. 25
4. 5
5. Either of the following: pineapple, canned, 78 calories—pineapple, fresh, 40 calories; or tomato, fresh, 40 calories—tomato juice, 50 calories—tomato soup, cream—175 calories
6. Any two of the following: applesauce, sweetened, 127 calories—applesauce, unsweetened, 50 calories; coffee, clear, 0 calories—coffee with 1 lump sugar, 180 calories; doughnut, plain, 165 calories—doughnut, sugared, 180 calories
7. chocolate malted milk (502 calories)
8. A lettuce and tomato sandwich on whole-wheat bread, with no butter or mayonnaise
9. Answers will vary.
10. Answers will vary.

Lesson 18

1 About the Scene

1. Answers will vary. Some students may feel that Ruth and Walter have a strong comfortable relationship, while others may think that their bickering is a symptom of a widening rift between them. Be sure students cite details that support their point of view.
2. Answers will vary. One possible answer is: She is strict but loving. She orders him to comb his hair and won't give him money for a cap, but she gives him a hug and words of playful affection.
3. Answers will vary. Accept any reasonable response.
4. Answers will vary. At the end of the play the family was moving to their own home. Ruth and Walter were expecting another baby and getting along better. However, since the entire play spans only a few weeks in their lives, any response that the student can justify is acceptable.

2 Synonyms and Antonyms

1. introduction, conclusion
2. sudden, slow
3. affection, dislike
4. exasperated, contented
5. comical, tragic
6. minimum, maximum
7. extend, compress
8. masculine, feminine
9. gleeful, dejected
10. extract, insert
11. average, remarkable
12. broad, narrow

3 Food for Thought

1. c	4. c	7. a	10. b	13. c
2. d	5. d	8. c	11. d	14. a
3. a	6. b	9. a	12. c	15. a

"brings home the bacon"

4 More Work with the Plural Possessive

1. cereal's, cereals'
2. frontiersman's, frontiersmen's
3. thief's, thieves'
4. foreigner's, foreigners'
5. utensil's, utensils'
6. child's, children's
7. McCormick's, McCormicks'
8. Congresswoman's, Congresswomen's
9. polisher's, polishers'
10. watermelon's, watermelons'
11. handyman's, handymen's
12. district's, districts'
13. reservation's, reservations'
14. axman's, axmen's
15. deer's, deer's

5 The Suffixes -ance and -ence

1. entrance	5. ignorance	9. confidence
2. annoyance	6. importance	10. riddance
3. substance	7. avoidance	
4. convenience	8. resistance	

Lesson 19

1 About the Reading

1. a	3. c	5. b	7. d	9. c
2. d	4. b	6. a	8. b	

2 What Do You Think?

1. Answers will vary. Accept any reasonable response.
2. Answers will vary.

3 A Taste Treat

Sweet
1. coffee cake
2. cream puffs
3. doughnuts
4. hot chocolate

Salty
1. bacon
2. corned beef
3. smoked ham
4. soy sauce

Bitter
1. baking chocolate
2. lemon peel
3. mustard greens
4. orange rind

Sour
1. grapefruit
2. lime juice
3. sauerkraut
4. vinegar

Answers to the last two questions will vary.

4 Word Families

1. nutritious, nutrition, nutrients
2. entertainer, entertainment, entertain
3. convenience, conveniently, convenient
4. practically, impractical, practical
5. possessive, possessed, possession
6. confidential, confided, confidence
7. created, creator, creation, creative
8. obey, obedience, obedient, obediently
9. scientist, science, scientifically, scientific
10. indifference, indifferently, indifferent

5 Review of the Apostrophe

1. cents' (second)	6. warrior's (first)
2. sausages' (second)	7. Joneses' (second)
3. Scientists' (first)	8. boy's (first)
4. days' (second)	9. noodles' (first)
5. trucker's (first)	10. emeralds' (second)

6 Can You Crack the Code?

1. emerald	5. topaz	9. amethyst
2. ruby	6. opal	10. garnet
3. pearl	7. sapphire	11. turquoise
4. diamond	8. bloodstone	12. sardonyx

Lesson 20

1 About the Reading

1. he seemed to have a magical ability to understand plants and to develop useful products from ordinary plants.
2. they were considered good only as food for hogs.
3. they had never heard of them.
4. he wanted to serve his own people.
5. he was dressed cheaply and didn't look or act important.
6. he didn't want to profit from God's gifts.
7. Any three of the following or similar examples: He rejected a job at Iowa State and went to Tuskegee instead. He turned down high-paying jobs with Edison and Ford. He didn't apply for patents for his discoveries. He wore two-dollar suits.
8. Answers will vary. Accept any reasonable response.
9. they didn't understand the source from which his magic with plants came.
10. they believed they could and loved the plants enough.

2 More Facts about the Peanut

pods, usually, unusual, groundnuts
plants, temperature, period, ripened, snap, Pegs
ripen, plows, soil, machines
harvested, per cent

3 Word Relationships

1. b	3. b	5. d	7. c	9. a
2. a	4. c	6. b	8. d	10. d

4 The Suffix -ize

1. specialize	5. memorize	9. terrorized
2. modernize	6. recognize	10. authorized
3. tenderized	7. organized	11. alphabetized
4. symbolizes	8. scandalized	12. criticize

5 Find This Peanut Product

1. nostril	6. gallbladder	11. raisin
2. inhale	7. laxative	12. infection
3. transfusion	8. yogurt	13. navel
4. ripcord	9. carbon dioxide	
5. oxygen	10. exhale	

The peanut product: nitroglycerin

6 To Look at Any Thing

1. Most of us see only the surface of things, only the most obvious details or characteristics.
2. We must look at it long and become the thing, taking plenty of time to imagine ourselves as being the thing we are seeing.
3. Carver said, "The secrets are in the plants. To learn them, you have to love them enough." Accept other reasonable examples.
4. Answers will vary. Reasonable responses include: Learn from nature; isolate yourself while you study the thing you want to really know; read the Bible.

Review: Lessons 1-20

1 Word Review

1. preservative	6. profession	11. compatibility
2. patent	7. utensil	12. transmission
3. wizard	8. inflation	13. tradition
4. nutrient	9. frontier	14. agriculture
5. miracle	10. blueprint	15. Senate

2 Which Word Does Not Fit?

1. Windbreaker	6. salary	11. valued
2. deserve	7. Los Angeles	12. stunning
3. numb	8. hardworking	13. turnip
4. Mediterranean	9. reject	14. Franklin
5. starvation	10. plague	15. gold

3 Word Study

1. Plagued, nagging, endure, whereupon, emergency
2. outraged, authorize, classified, creative, opportunities
3. scientist, assumed, concocted, assistant, explanation
4. advice, devise, device, advised, revise
5. desperate, dutiful, oppression, injected, fowl
6. formally, formerly, confident, envy, detract
7. minimum, accommodate, maximum, limit, resume
8. unlike, unknown, unpleasant, unusually, unfruitful

4 Review of Compound Words

1. b	4. a	7. b	10. b
2. b	5. c	8. a	11. c
3. d	6. a	9. a	12. c

5 Review of Contractions

1. he's	8. won't	15. there's
2. they'll	9. she's	16. she'd
3. doesn't	10. you'll	17. I'm
4. we've	11. don't	18. let's
5. you'd	12. I'll	19. he'd
6. I'd	13. what's	20. ma'am
7. hadn't	14. they'd	

6 Review of Facts and Opinions

1. fact	5. opinion	9. fact
2. fact	6. fact	10. opinion
3. opinion	7. fact	11. fact
4. fact	8. fact	12. opinion

Word Indexes for Book 6

Word Index: Lessons 1-5

A
abdomen
ability
actress
Adam
advancement
adventure
adventurous
adventurously
ailment
airport
Alaska
almanac
ancestor
Andrew
angrily
appear
appearance
arithmetic
assist
assistance
assistant
association
attachment
audience
awareness

B
backhand
bitterness
blackjack
bloodiness
blot
boo
bookkeeper
bottleneck
breakneck

C
calendar
caliber
calmness
camera
Canada
Canadian
capitalization
Capitol
cave-in
ceaselessly
celluloid
central
checker
checkerboard
Cherokee

cinema
classical
clockwork
clumsiness
cold-eyed
colored
Columbia
commitment
compartment
concealment
concentrate
concentration
confinement
Congress
consider
construction
continuous
continuously
Cooper, J.
cornea
cornerstone
costume
crackly
craziness
crookneck
curiously

D
democratic
depth
description
desperate
desperately
desperation
destruction
detachment
dialogue
diameter
direction
director
dirtiness
disappear
disappearance
discouragement
dislike
displeasure
dizziness
dry-eyed
dryness
duct
dullness
dustiness

E
eagerly
eagerness
earache
employment
encouragement
engagement
enjoyment
enlargement
Europe
event
eyeball
eyelid

F
faultiness
favorite
fireworks
fluid
fondness
Ford
forgetfulness
forgiveness
formerly
foul
freshness
funeral

G
gadabout
gentleness
getaway
get-together
Good Friday
govern
government
governor
gracefulness
greasiness
greatness
gunfight
gunfighter
gunplay

H
habit
happening
hardness
hatred
Hawaiian
headache
headstone
heartily
Hickok, J.

historical
hitchhiker
holiness
holler
Hollywood
holster
housekeeper

I
image
imagination
imagine
industry
inelastic
inkblot
insecure
insistence
inspection
instance
institution
instruction
instructor
involvement
irregular
itchiness

J
Jackie
Jackson
Jackson, A.
Jesse

K
knowledge

L
Lansing
lasting
leftovers
lens
liberty
Life Saver
liveliness
loudness
loveliness

M
management
manpower
measure
measurement
medical
merrily
merry

Mexico
millimeter
misplacement
Mississippi
mistreatment
monster
mother-in-law

N
Nashville
nastiness
national
nationality
needlework
Negro
New Orleans
noisiness
Norman
North Carolina
nosiness
nowadays

O
occur
occurrence
oddball
offspring
officeholder
Oklahoma
Oklahoma City
Ontario
operate
operation
operator
organization
outclass
outdated
outfit
outgoing
outlive
outspoken
overhand
owl

P
passing
performance
persistence
persistent
persistently
playhouse
pleasantly
plumpness
politely

politeness
political
popular
position
product
projection
projector
protection
protector
protest
province
punishment

Q

R
raring
reality
receiver
recently
regular
repairman
requirement
research
resent
resentful
resentfully
resentment
retirement
reviewer
riskiness
riverside
roach
Roger
Rogers, W.
roundabout
rudeness
runabout

S
saddle
saltiness
Salt Lake City
sandman
sandstone
scene
scratchiness
secondhand
secure
securely
security
separate
serious
seriously
seriousness
settlement
shipment

shooter
shopkeeper
short-lived
showdown
shutter
sightseeing
silence
sinfulness
sleepiness
smartly
smoothness
sneakiness
softness
South Carolina
special
spiciness
Springfield
stalk
standard
standby
standout
standpoint
statue
stiffness
stillness
stomachache
storekeeper
suffix
support
Supreme Court

T
tantrum
tastelessness
Technicolor
tenderly
tendon
theater
thirstiness
thunderbolt
thundercloud
thundershower
thunderstorm
timecard
timekeeper
timepiece
timetable
timework
toothache
travel
Trenton
truthfulness
turnabout
turtleneck

U
ugliness
underclothes
underside
uneasily
uneasiness
unharmed
university
unpleasantly
unpopular
unused
unwanted
upbringing
U.S.
usefulness
uselessness
usually

V
vessel
victim
viewer

W
wallop
warmly
wastefulness
weightlifter
well-mannered
width
wonderment
World Series

X
X-rated

Y
yellowish
yelp

Z

Word Index: Lessons 6-10

A
abbreviation
Abraham
abuse
activity
actual
actually
Adams, J. Q.
addition
adjust
adjustment
advertise
advertisement
advise
aftertaste
ageless
agency
agent
airline
Alabama
Allah
all-time
alphabetize
applicant
application
apply
artist
ashamed
attention
attitude
availability
available

B
Baptist
bareness
barmaid
barrel
beaver
beekeeper
behold
benefit
bitterly
blameless
bookkeeping
brakeman
brass
broker
Buddha
butcher

C
Campbell
carpentry
caseworker
certificate
chapter

checkmate
cheerily
childless
Christianity
churchyard
circumstance
classification
classified
classify
college
coma
concrete
congressman
consist
contact
contentment
cookout
corncob
couple
cowardliness
cowardly
cowpuncher
crazily
create
creative
crisis
crossbones
current
currently

D
delicately
delightfully
dependable
dependent
deposit
desirable
dictate
difficulty
directly
disability
dismiss
dismissal
doubtfully
dreamily
dutiful

E
earner
elect
election
emotionally
enroll
eventful
exam
examine
excellent

experience
experiment
ex-president

F
faithfully
fearful
fearfully
fearless
fearlessly
federal
felony
fiddlesticks
fierce
fisher
floorwalker
flunk
forceful
forcefully
forecaster
foreman
formally
fortieth
Francis
freeloader
furthermore
fury

G
gangplank
general
generally
gladness
gracefully
graduate
greenwood
grindstone
guarantee
guiltily

H
hassle
haystack
heartiness
heartless
heartlessly
hearty
hereby
herein
hillside
Hiram
honestly
housewarming

I
idle
immediate

immediately
impolite
impolitely
impression
incorrectly
increasingly
indicate
individual
individually
information
innocence
innocent
innocently
inspiration
instrument
interview
interviewer
investigate
Isaac
Islam
Italian

J
Jane
Japanese
Jefferson, T.
jew's-harp
Joe
Judaism
judgment
Justin

K
Kennedy, J. F.
Koran

L
legal
legally
lest
level
lifelong
lightning
limitless
Lincoln, A.
listener
locksmith
lollipop
lookout
loosely
loser
lumberjack

M
machinery
Madison, J.
madman

magazine
magically
major
manhood
marble
masterpiece
McCarthy
meaningless
means
meanwhile
merciful
merciless
merriment
Messiah
Mick
middleman
mightily
military
mindless
mindlessly
minor
misjudgment
mixture
Monroe, J.
moodily
moosewood
Mormon
mouthwash
multiply
mutter

N
nab
namely
neatness
needful
negative
negatively
North American
nursemaid

O
occupation
omission
origin
out-and-out
overwork

P
particular
particularly
parachute
passenger
Peggy
penknife
perfectly
pimple

plank
plateful
policewoman
Polk, J.
Polly
popularly
positive
positively
possess
possession
precisely
prefer
preference
prefix
presser
previous
previously
prisoner
privately
prom
promise
promote
psychiatrist
pure
purely

Q

quality
questioning
questioningly
Quincy

R

rape
razor
realistic
realistically
reckon
redden
reference
referral
register
regretful
regretfully
religion
religious
regularly
rental
response
responsibility
responsible
resume
rewritten
Richard
right-hand
Ritz
Robert

rock-bottom
roll call

S

salary
salesclerk
sawyer
scatterbrain
scoopful
scorn
scornful
scornfully
screenwriter
seam
seasick
separately
setter
shamefully
shameless
Sherman
shoplifter
shucks
signature
signpost
sixteenth
slaveholder
slavery
slipperiness
slippery
slowness
slyness
social
socially
soldier
solution
sorrowfully
spirit
sportswear
squeamishly
staircase
stake
stationmaster
steadily
steamboat
stockbroker
stockroom
stubborn
stubbornly
stubbornness
stump
stupidly
succeed
suicide
supervisor
survey
symbol

T

tadpole
talent
Talmud
terrify
Terry
testament
thoughtlessly
timber
title
tomb
topmost
tractor
transportation
trickle
Twain, M.
typesetter
typing

U

uncertainly
Uncle Sam
underpaid
undertook
undesirable
unemployment
union
unite
United Nations
unlike
unload
unpleasant
unstructured
untried
unusual
unusually
unwillingness
unworthily
unworthy
unwritten
usefully
uselessly
usual

V

vague
vaguely
vagueness
vastly
vastness
victory
viewpoint
volunteer

W

wagon
walker

wallflower
ward
warmth
warship
waterfront
we'd
whiten
whitewash
worldly
worthily

X

Y

Z

Word Index: Lessons 11-15

A
abbreviate
aboard
absorber
accommodate
acid
adder
addiction
adrift
adventurer
air-condition
aircraft
alphabetical
Amazon
amnesia
anchor
angel
announce
announcement
Anthony
Apollo
apostrophe
appeal
apron
Arctic Ocean
ashore
assign
assume
astronaut
attempt
attendant
attract
average
axman

B
backstage
barbershop
bay
Betsy
biscuit
bleat
blindfold
bowstring
bra
breaker
Broadway
Brooklyn
bulletin

C
cabman
candlelight
canvas
capsule
captain
Caribbean
carriage

cartoonist
Challenger
chief
chimney
chubby
churchgoing
CIA
clothe
compass
compliment
compress
conflict
Connecticut
conscious
consciousness
conserve
consideration
contend
contradiction
contradict
coonskin
cosmonaut
criminal
cross-town
Cupid

D
daredevil
decrease
defense
dental
design
detract
device
devil
devise
discard
distance
district
distrust
dutifully

E
easel
eastward
electricity
emergency
encyclopedia
endless
entertainment
envy
evidence
expensive
extract

F
far-reaching

FBI
fiftieth
firearm
flier
forearm
fortune
Franklin
frivol
furniture

G
gallop
gangway
garage
gather
gay
generation
geographical
giant
gloomily
glorious
Great Salt Lake
guesswork

H
handyman
heavenly
heavily
heavyweight
Henry
horseless
homecoming

I
illegal
impatient
impatiently
importance
imprison
increasing
indeed
independent
indigestion
indirect
inexpensive
inexperience
inexperienced
instant
introduce
introduction
irresponsible
IRS

J
Jacuzzi
junior

K
Kelly

kerosene
knead

L
Lake Louise
launch
lengthen
life belt
liftoff
liquor
livelihood
livelong
long-winded
lottery

M
mango
Manhattan
manipulator
manmade
Mediterranean
megaphone
memory
minimum
modern
Molly
moor
morphine
moth-eaten
motor
motorboat
motorcar
motorcycle
motorist
motorman
mph
myth
mythology

N
naked
NASA
natural
nearness
nephew
nerveless
nonmetal
nonskid
North Sea
northwestern
Norwegian

O
oarsman
oilskin
opinion
orbit
overview
ownership

P
Pacific
pantsuit
partly
passage
patient
peacock
Pennsylvania
pierce
pilot
pilothouse
planner
plentiful
poll
popularity
poverty
precook
predate
preheat
prehistory
prejudge
premedical
prepay
preschool
preserve
preshrunk
pretest
prewar
privacy
progress
proven
provide
publisher
purchase

Q

R
radiator
rascal
rather
rebuild
reckless
reclaim
reconsider
reconstruct
reconstruction
recount
redouble
refit
refuel
regain
rein
relay
remote
reopen
reorganization

repeated
rephrase
replant
repossess
rerun
reserve
resourceful
retrace
retrieve
reunion
revise
revoke
revolution
rider
rifle
ripcord
roadwork
roommate
rosebush
routine
ruin
ruins
Russian

S
sag
Sally
satellite
self-governing
self-interest
self-starter
self-supporting
servant
setback
sextant
shapeless
sheepishly
she'll
shorten
shovel
shuttle
snobbish
snobbishness
sober
society
soot
source
Soviet
Soviet Union
spacecraft
spitefully
spotlight
sputter
staff
steamer
stint
stow

stun
submit
subtract
supervise
supply
surface
survivor
suspect

T
tentmaker
thunderous
tie-up
tightwad
till
tombstone
tragic
transmit
traveler
tuna

U
unclothed
undisturbed
unending
unexpected
unfasten
unfeeling
unfruitful
ungrateful
unhurt
uninformed
uninterested
unknot
unlimited
unloose
unsheltered
unskilled
unsolved
untrue

V
vehicle
veterinary
Volkswagen
voyage
voyager

W
wad
wardrobe
Warsaw
waterproof
watertight
weapon
weave
Wendy

westerly
wildness
Windbreaker
windshield

X

Y
year-round
yield

Z

Word Index: Lessons 16-20

A

abruptly
absently
accommodation
account
adapt
admittance
adventuresome
advisor
affair
affection
agricultural
agriculture
Alexis
alike
amethyst
annoyance
applejack
Appleseed, J.
approach
artificial
attendance
authorize
automatic
automatically
avoidance
await
axle

B

backdrop
banana
basic
Beaumont
bellybutton
beloved
Betty
blackout
bloodstone
blueprint
bonehead
Boxer
breathlessly
broad
brownout
brownstone
busload
by-product

C

calorie
campaign
canned
cannery
Capitol Hill
caretaker
casserole

CB
century
cereal
Chapman, J.
cherrystone
chuckhole
Civil War
clever
colonel
colonist
colony
colorless
comical
comically
committee
community
compatibility
composition
conclusion
concoct
concussion
confession
confidence
confident
confidently
confusion
congresswoman
constipation
convenience
convenient
conveniently
convert
cosmetics
crackerjack
cream puff
creation
creator
criticize
crunchy
cultural

D

dairy
definition
deliver
dependence
diarrhea
digestive
disadvantage
disbelief
disobedience
disorder
dissolve
distant
disturbance
division
Donald

doorstep
downswing
downturn
drawback
drily
dynamite

E

educated
eighteenth
element
embrace
emerald
Emory
emphasis
enable
endurance
endure
entertain
entertainer
entitle
entrance
especially
everyday
exasperate
excellence
exhaustion
explanation
extension
extraction

F

faithfulness
famous
feminine
ferny
finding
first-class
flavor
flavorful
floodlight
foolproof
foreign
foreigner
fray
freckle
fritter
frontier
frontiersman
frustrate
frustration
fulfill
function

G

gallstone
gangster

garnet
gaslight
gemstone
Girl Scout
gleeful
gleefully
graduation
granola
grapevine
graze
greenback
groundnut
groundwork
grove
grudgingly
gruffness

H

handicraft
harden
harvest
hash
hash house
healthful
heartburn
Helen
Hershey
hog
homeroom
homestretch
honesty
hunchback

I

ignorance
imaginary
impractical
Inc.
inconvenience
independence
Indiana
indifference
indifferent
indifferently
infection
inflation
influence
inject
injection
insecticide
insert
instep
invasion
investigation
investor

J

jade
Jay
JoAnne
Johnny

K

L

label
laboratory
largely
laundryman
laxative
lemonade
lengthy
limelight
local
location
lowly
Luella

M

macaroni
magician
mainland
mainspring
mainstay
mainstream
mangle
manly
Marsha
masculine
masculinity
material
maximum
McCormick
mechanically
medium
memorize
meter
method
miracle
Missouri
modernize
mulberry
mumps
mysterious

N

native
naturally
navel
necessarily
ninth
nitroglycerin
noodle

nutrient
nutrition
nutritional
nutritious

O

obedience
obedient
obediently
odorless
opal
oppression
orchard
organist
organize
original
output
outrage
overrule
overtake
oz.

P

pajamas
pare
patent
patiently
peephole
peg
Pepsi
phonograph
picket
pineapple
plague
playfulness
plentifully
plume
polisher
population
portray
possessive
practical
practically
presentation
preservative
production
profession
profit
pudding
putter

Q

R

raisin
raspberry

readily
redhead
reinsert
remarkable
repeatedly
represent
researcher
reservation
resistance
resourcefulness
revision
rhubarb
riddance
rightly
ripen
ripeness
Rosella

S

sapphire
sardonyx
sauerkraut
sausage
scandalize
science
scientific
scientifically
scientist
sear
secret
self-taught
Senate
settler
sewing
simply
sinner
snub
so-called
sometime
specialize
spoilage
starvation
steeplejack
stiffly
St. Martin
store-bought
striker
stunning
stunningly
substance
sugarplum
supernatural
supervision
surroundings
sweeten
sweet potato
symbolize

T

tailback
temporary
temptation
tenderize
terrorize
testify
therein
topaz
topsoil
tradition
transfer
transform
transfusion
transmission
transport
tribune
trucker
turquoise
Tuskegee
typical

U

undigested
unexplained
unhappily
unknown
unleash
unnatural
unnaturally
unsweetened
unwaxed
utensil

V

variety
vice president
viciously
village
villager
vinegar
visitor
vitamin

W

wanderer
warrior
Washington, B. T.
watermelon
weaver
well-being
westward
whereas
whereupon
whiteout
whole-wheat
wicker

Willard
Willy
witchcraft
wizard
woodcraft
worsen
worthlessness
wrestling
wrongly

X

Y

youngster

Z

Word Index: Lessons 1-20

A

abbreviate
abbreviation
abdomen
ability
aboard
Abraham
abruptly
absently
absorber
abuse
accommodate
accommodation
account
acid
activity
actress
actual
actually
Adam
Adams, J. Q.
adapt
adder
addiction
addition
adjust
adjustment
admittance
adrift
advancement
adventure
adventurer
adventuresome
adventurous
adventurously
advertise
advertisement
advise
advisor
affair
affection
aftertaste
ageless
agency
agent
agricultural
agriculture
ailment
air-condition
aircraft
airline
airport
Alabama
Alaska
Alexis
alike
Allah

all-time
almanac
alphabetical
alphabetize
Amazon
amethyst
amnesia
ancestor
anchor
Andrew
angel
angrily
announce
announcement
annoyance
Anthony
Apollo
apostrophe
appeal
appear
appearance
applejack
Appleseed, J.
applicant
application
apply
approach
apron
Arctic Ocean
arithmetic
artificial
artist
ashamed
ashore
assign
assist
assistance
assistant
association
assume
astronaut
attachment
attempt
attendance
attendant
attention
attitude
attract
audience
authorize
automatic
automatically
availability
available
average
avoidance
await

awareness
axle
axman

B

backdrop
backhand
backstage
banana
Baptist
barbershop
bareness
barmaid
barrel
basic
bay
Beaumont
beaver
beekeeper
behold
bellybutton
beloved
benefit
Betsy
Betty
biscuit
bitterly
bitterness
blackjack
blackout
blameless
bleat
blindfold
bloodiness
bloodstone
blot
blueprint
bonehead
boo
bookkeeper
bookkeeping
bottleneck
bowstring
Boxer
bra
brakeman
brass
breaker
breakneck
breathlessly
broad
Broadway
broker
Brooklyn
brownout
brownstone
Buddah

bulletin
busload
butcher
by-product

C

cabman
calendar
caliber
calmness
calorie
camera
campaign
Campbell
Canada
Canadian
candlelight
canned
cannery
canvas
capitalization
Capitol
Capitol Hill
capsule
captain
caretaker
Caribbean
carpentry
carriage
cartoonist
caseworker
casserole
cave-in
CB
ceaselessly
celluloid
central
century
cereal
certificate
Challenger
Chapman, J.
chapter
checker
checkerboard
checkmate
cheerily
Cherokee
cherrystone
chief
childless
chimney
Christianity
chubby
chuckhole
churchgoing
churchyard

CIA
cinema
circumstance
Civil War
classical
classification
classified
classify
clever
clockwork
clothe
clumsiness
cold-eyed
college
colonel
colonist
colony
colored
colorless
Columbia
coma
comical
comically
commitment
committee
community
compartment
compass
compatibility
compliment
composition
compress
concealment
concentrate
concentration
conclusion
concoct
concrete
concussion
confession
confidence
confident
confidently
confinement
conflict
confusion
Congress
congressman
congresswoman
Connecticut
conscious
consciousness
conserve
consider
consideration
consist
constipation

construction
contact
contend
contentment
continuous
continuously
contraction
contradict
convenience
convenient
conveniently
convert
cookout
coonskin
Cooper, J.
corncob
cornea
cornerstone
cosmetics
cosmonaut
costume
couple
cowardliness
cowardly
cowpuncher
crackerjack
crackly
crazily
craziness
cream puff
create
creation
creative
creator
criminal
crisis
criticize
crookneck
crossbones
cross-town
crunchy
cultural
Cupid
curiously
current
currently

D

dairy
daredevil
decrease
defense
definition
delicately
delightfully
deliver

democratic
dental
dependable
dependence
dependent
deposit
depth
description
design
desirable
desperate
desperately
desperation
destruction
detachment
detract
device
devil
devise
dialogue
diameter
diarrhea
dictate
difficulty
digestive
direction
directly
director
dirtiness
disability
disadvantage
disappear
disappearance
disbelief
discard
discouragement
dislike
dismiss
dismissal
disobedience
disorder
displeasure
dissolve
distance
distant
district
distrust
disturbance
division
dizziness
Donald
doorstep
doubtfully
downswing
downturn
drawback
dreamily

drily
dry-eyed
dryness
duct
dullness
dustiness
dutiful
dutifully
dynamite

E

eagerly
eagerness
earache
earner
easel
eastward
educated
eighteenth
elect
election
electricity
element
embrace
emerald
emergency
Emory
emotionally
emphasis
employment
enable
encouragement
encyclopedia
endless
endurance
endure
engagement
enjoyment
enlargement
enroll
entertain
entertainer
entertainment
entitle
entrance
envy
especially
Europe
event
eventful
everyday
evidence
exam
examine
exasperate
excellence
excellent

exhaustion
expensive
experience
experiment
explanation
ex-president
extension
extract
extraction
eyeball
eyelid

F

faithfully
faithfulness
famous
far-reaching
faultiness
favorite
FBI
fearful
fearfully
fearless
fearlessly
federal
felony
feminine
ferny
fiddlesticks
fierce
fiftieth
finding
firearm
fireworks
first-class
fisher
flavor
flavorful
flier
floodlight
floorwalker
fluid
flunk
foolproof
fondness
forceful
forcefully
Ford
forearm
forecaster
foreign
foreigner
foreman
forgetfulness
forgiveness
formally

formerly
fortieth
fortune
foul
Francis
Franklin
fray
freckle
freeloader
freshness
fritter
frivol
frontier
frontiersman
frustrate
frustration
fulfill
function
funeral
furniture
furthermore
fury

G

gadabout
gallop
gallstone
gangplank
gangster
gangway
garage
garnet
gaslight
gather
gay
gemstone
general
generally
generation
gentleness
geographical
getaway
get-together
giant
Girl Scout
gladness
gleeful
gleefully
gloomily
glorious
Good Friday
govern
government
governor
gracefully
gracefulness
graduate

graduation
granola
grapevine
graze
greasiness
greatness
Great Salt Lake
greenback
greenwood
grindstone
groundnut
groundwork
grove
grudgingly
gruffness
guarantee
guesswork
guiltily
gunfight
gunfighter
gunplay

H
habit
handicraft
handyman
happening
harden
hardness
harvest
hash
hash house
hassle
hatred
Hawaiian
haystack
headache
headstone
healthful
heartburn
heartily
heartiness
heartless
heartlessly
hearty
heavenly
heavily
heavyweight
Helen
Henry
hereby
herein
Hershey
Hickok, J.
hillside
Hiram
historical

hitchhiker
hog
holiness
holler
Hollywood
holster
homecoming
homeroom
homestretch
honestly
honesty
horseless
housekeeper
housewarming
hunchback

I
idle
ignorance
illegal
image
imaginary
imagination
imagine
immediate
immediately
impatient
impatiently
impolite
impolitely
importance
impractical
impression
imprison
Inc.
inconvenience
incorrectly
increasing
increasingly
indeed
independence
independent
Indiana
indicate
indifference
indifferent
indifferently
indigestion
indirect
individual
individually
industry
inelastic
inexpensive
inexperience

inexperienced
infection
inflation
influence
information
inject
injection
inkblot
innocence
innocent
innocently
insecticide
insecure
insert
insistence
inspection
inspiration
instance
instant
instep
institution
instruction
instructor
instrument
interview
interviewer
introduce
introduction
invasion
investigate
investigation
investor
involvement
irregular
irresponsible
IRS
Isaac
Islam
Italian
itchiness

J
Jackie
Jackson
Jackson, A.
Jacuzzi
jade
Jane
Japanese
Jay
Jefferson, T.
Jesse
jew's-harp
JoAnne
Joe
Johnny

Judaism
judgment
junior
Justin

K
Kelly
Kennedy, J. F.
kerosene
knead
knowledge
Koran

L
label
laboratory
Lake Louise
Lansing
largely
lasting
launch
laundryman
laxative
leftovers
legal
legally
lemonade
lengthen
lengthy
lens
lest
level
liberty
life belt
lifelong
Life Saver
liftoff
lightning
limelight
limitless
Lincoln, A.
liquor
listener
livelihood
liveliness
livelong
local
location
locksmith
lollipop
long-winded
lookout
loosely
loser
lottery
loudness

loveliness
lowly
Luella
lumberjack

M
macaroni
machinery
Madison, J.
madman
magazine
magically
magician
mainland
mainspring
mainstay
mainstream
major
management
mangle
mango
Manhattan
manhood
manipulator
manly
manmade
manpower
marble
Marsha
masculine
masculinity
masterpiece
material
maximum
McCarthy
McCormick
meaningless
means
meanwhile
measure
measurement
mechanically
medical
Mediterranean
medium
megaphone
memorize
memory
merciful
merciless
merrily
merriment
merry
Messiah
meter
method
Mexico

Mick
middleman
mightily
military
millimeter
mindless
mindlessly
minimum
minor
miracle
misjudgment
misplacement
Mississippi
Missouri
mistreatment
mixture
modern
modernize
Molly
Monroe, J.
monster
moodily
moor
moosewood
Mormon
morphine
moth-eaten
mother-in-law
motor
motorboat
motorcar
motorcycle
motorist
motorman
mouthwash
mph
mulberry
multiply
mumps
mutter
mysterious
myth
mythology

N
nab
naked
namely
NASA
Nashville
nastiness
national
nationality
native
natural
naturally
navel

nearness
neatness
necessarily
needful
needlework
negative
negatively
Negro
nephew
nerveless
New Orleans
ninth
nitroglycerin
noisiness
nonmetal
nonskid
noodle
Norman
North American
North Carolina
North Sea
northwestern
Norwegian
nosiness
nowadays
nursemaid
nutrient
nutrition
nutritional
nutritious

O
oarsman
obedience
obedient
obediently
occupation
occur
occurrence
oddball
odorless
officeholder
offspring
oilskin
Oklahoma
Oklahoma City
omission
Ontario
opal
operate
operation
operator
opinion
oppression
orbit
orchard

organist
organization
organize
origin
original
out-and-out
outclass
outdated
outfit
outgoing
outlive
output
outrage
outspoken
overhand
overrule
overtake
overview
overwork
owl
ownership
oz.

P
Pacific
pajamas
pantsuit
parachute
pare
particular
particularly
partly
passage
passenger
passing
patent
patient
patiently
peacock
peephole
peg
Peggy
penknife
Pennsylvania
Pepsi
perfectly
performance
persistence
persistent
persistently
phonograph
picket
pierce
pilot
pilothouse
pimple
pineapple

plague
plank
planner
plateful
playfulness
playhouse
pleasantly
plentiful
plentifully
plume
plumpness
policewoman
polisher
politely
politeness
political
Polk, J.
poll
Polly
popular
popularity
popularly
population
portray
position
positive
positively
possess
possession
possessive
poverty
practical
practically
precisely
precook
predate
prefer
preference
prefix
preheat
prehistory
prejudge
premedical
prepay
preschool
presentation
preservative
preserve
preshrunk
presser
pretest
previous
previously
prewar
prisoner
privacy
privately

product
production
profession
profit
progress
projection
projector
prom
promise
promote
protection
protector
protest
proven
provide
province
psychiatrist
publisher
pudding
punishment
purchase
pure
purely
putter

Q
quality
questioning
questioningly
Quincy

R
radiator
raisin
rape
raring
rascal
raspberry
rather
razor
readily
realistic
realistically
reality
rebuild
receiver
recently
reckless
reckon
reclaim
reconsider
reconstruct
reconstruction
recount
redden
redhead
redouble

reference
referral
refit
refuel
regain
register
regretful
regretfully
regular
regularly
rein
reinsert
relay
religion
religious
remarkable
remote
rental
reopen
reorganization
repairman
repeated
repeatedly
rephrase
replant
repossess
represent
requirement
rerun
research
researcher
resent
resentful
resentfully
resentment
reservation
reserve
resistance
resourceful
resourcefulness
response
responsibility
responsible
resume
retirement
retrace
retrieve
reunion
reviewer
revise
revision
revoke
revolution
rewritten
rhubarb
Richard
riddance

rider
rifle
right-hand
rightly
ripcord
ripen
ripeness
riskiness
Ritz
riverside
roach
roadwork
Robert
rock-bottom
Roger
Rogers, W.
roll call
roommate
rosebush
Rosella
roundabout
routine
rudeness
ruin
ruins
runabout
Russian

S

saddle
sag
salary
salesclerk
Sally
saltiness
Salt Lake City
sandman
sandstone
sapphire
sardonyx
satellite
sauerkraut
sausage
sawyer
scandalize
scatterbrain
scene
science
scientific
scientifically
scientist
scoopful
scorn
scornful
scornfully
scratchiness

screenwriter
seam
sear
seasick
secondhand
secret
secure
securely
security
self-governing
self-interest
self-starter
self-supporting
self-taught
Senate
separate
separately
series
serious
seriously
seriousness
servant
setback
setter
settlement
settler
sewing
sextant
shamefully
shameless
shapeless
sheepishly
she'll
Sherman
shipment
shooter
shopkeeper
shoplifter
shorten
short-lived
shovel
showdown
shucks
shutter
shuttle
sightseeing
signature
signpost
silence
simply
sinfulness
sinner
sixteenth
slaveholder
slavery
sleepiness
slipperiness

slippery
slowness
slyness
smartly
smoothness
sneakiness
snobbish
snobbishness
snub
sober
so-called
social
socially
society
softness
soldier
solution
sometime
soot
sorrowfully
source
South Carolina
Soviet
Soviet Union
spacecraft
special
specialize
spiciness
spirit
spitefully
spoilage
sportswear
spotlight
Springfield
sputter
squeamishly
staff
staircase
stake
stalk
standard
standby
standout
standpoint
starvation
stationmaster
statue
steadily
steamboat
steamer
steeplejack
stiffly
stiffness
stillness
stint
St. Martin
stockbroker

stockroom
stomachache
store-bought
storekeeper
stow
striker
stubborn
stubbornly
stubbornness
stump
stun
stunning
stunningly
stupidly
submit
substance
subtract
succeed
suffix
sugarplum
suicide
supermarket
supernatural
supervise
supervision
supervisor
supply
support
Supreme Court
surface
surroundings
survey
survivor
suspect
sweeten
sweet potato
symbol
symbolize

T

tadpole
tailback
talent
Talmud
tantrum
tastelessness
Technicolor
temporary
temptation
tenderize
tenderly
tendon
tentmaker
terrify
terrorize
Terry
testament

testify
theater
therein
thirstiness
thoughtlessly
thunderbolt
thundercloud
thunderous
thundershower
thunderstorm
tie-up
tightwad
till
timber
timecard
timekeeper
timepiece
timetable
timework
title
tomb
tombstone
toothache
topaz
topmost
topsoil
tractor
tradition
tragic
transfer
transform
transfusion
transmission
transmit
transport
transportation
travel
traveler
Trenton
tribune
trickle
trucker
truthfulness
tuna
turnabout
turquoise
turtleneck
Tuskegee
Twain, M.
typesetter
typical
typing

U

ugliness
uncertainly
Uncle Sam

unclothed
underclothes
underpaid
underside
undertook
undesirable
undigested
undisturbed
uneasily
uneasiness
unemployment
unending
unexpected
unexplained
unfasten
unfeeling
unfruitful
ungrateful
unhappily
unharmed
unhurt
uninformed
uninterested
union
unite
United Nations
university
unknot
unknown
unleash
unlike
unlimited
unload
unloose
unnatural
unnaturally
unpleasant
unpleasantly
unpopular
unsheltered
unskilled
unsolved
unstructured
unsweetened
untried
untrue
unused
unusual
unusually
unwanted
unwaxed
unwillingness
unworthily
unworthy
unwritten
upbringing
U.S.

usefully
usefulness
uselessly
uselessness
usual
usually
utensil

V

vague
vaguely
vagueness
variety
vastly
vastness
vehicle
vessel
veterinary
vice president
viciously
victim
victory
viewer
viewpoint
village
villager
vinegar
visitor
vitamin
Volkswagen
volunteer
voyage
voyager

W

wad
wagon
walker
wallflower
wallop
wanderer
ward
wardrobe
warmly
warmth
warrior
Warsaw
warship
Washington, B. T.
wastefulness
waterfront
watermelon
waterproof
watertight
weapon
weave
weaver

we'd
weightlifter
well-being
well-mannered
Wendy
westerly
westward
whereas
whereupon
whiten
whiteout
whitewash
whole-wheat
wicker
width
wildness
Willard
Willy
Windbreaker
windshield
witchcraft
wizard
wonderment
woodcraft
worldly
World Series
worsen
worthily
worthlessness
wrestling
wrongly

X

X-rated

Y

year-round
yellowish
yelp
yield
youngster

Z